TOTTENHAM HOTSPUR

FA Cup Scrapbook 1901

Spurs First Cup

Previous Publications in the "Scrapbook" series:
Bradford City Season Scrapbook 1903/04 – Crossing Codes
Bradford City Season Scrapbook 1907/08 – Second Division Champions.
Bradford Park Avenue Season Scrapbook 1907/08 – A Southern Adventure
Leeds Utd Season Scrapbook 1919/20-20/21 – From the Ashes
Preston North End Season Scrapbook 1888/89 – The Invincibles
Bradford City F.A. Cup Scrapbook 1911 – How t'Cup Came Home to Bradford

Tottenham Hotspur

FA Cup Scrapbook 1901
Spurs First Cup

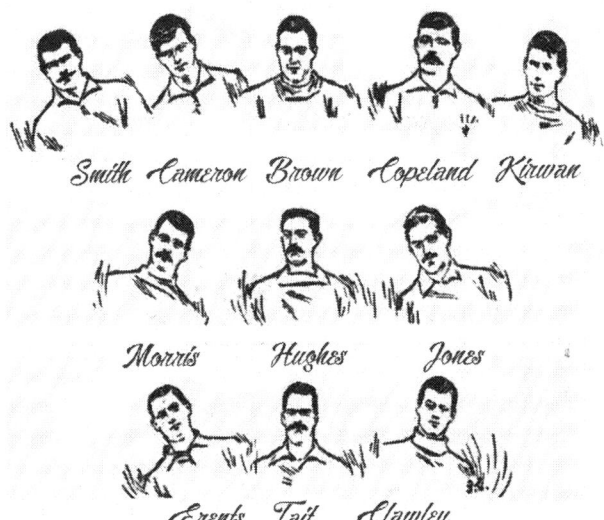

Published by Don Gillan – MMXVII – Rev 1.03
Copyright © Don Gillan, January 2018 – All rights reserved.

Manuscript created entirely in Libre Office
the World's most powerful FREE office productivity suite
https://www.libreoffice.org/

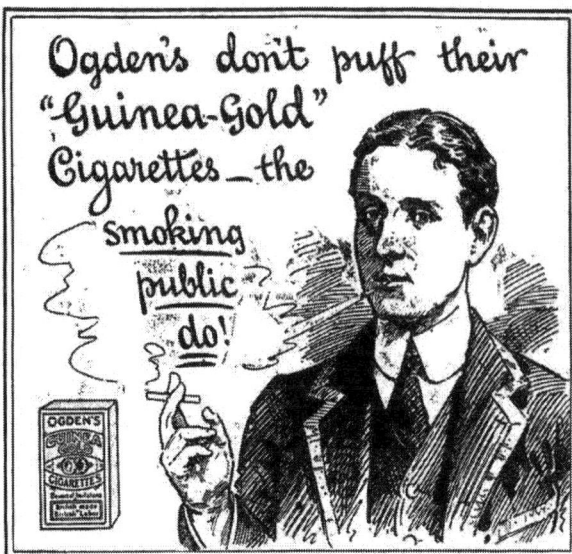

F. H. AYRES,
MANUFACTURER OF BILLIARD TABLES.

John Roberts made his RECORD BREAK OF 679, Spot and Push-barred, on a BILLIARD TABLE MADE by F. H. AYRES.

This Table has been SPECIALLY DESIGNED and MANUFACTURED for LICENSED VICTUALLERS with "INTERNATIONAL LOW FAST CUSHIONS," ALL LATEST IMPROVEMENTS, and MASSIVE SOLID MAHOGANY LEGS.

PRICE LIST ON APPLICATION.

111, ALDERSGATE-STREET, LONDON, E.C.

[COPY.] Ye Olde Red Lion, Islington, October 11, 1900.
F. H. Ayres, Esq., 111, Aldersgate-street, London.
DEAR SIR,—We have much pleasure in stating that the two Billiard Tables you supplied to us have proved very satisfactory. Also that the players at the "Licensed Victuallers" Tournament, held at the above address, all testified to the excellence of the Billiard Tables. Mr Diggle, the well-known player, when playing Mr G. Sala (Champion of Scotland) on one of those tables informed Mr Dickerson that it was one of the best Billiard Tables he had ever played on.—Yours truly,
(Signed), DICKERSON and NORTH.

FOREWORD

By almost any reckoning, Tottenham Hotspur are, at the time of writing (2017), ranked among the top 20 most prominent clubs in the Football world. Forbes, for example, ranked the 'Spurs as the 10th most valuable club in the world, whilst Deloitte, using slightly different criteria, ranked them twelfth. U.E.F.A.'s performance based ranking, meanwhile, placed 'Spurs 20th in Europe - still highly meritorious but, perhaps, in light of the former, indicative of recent under achievement.

In the light of the 'Spurs current standing it is easy to forget that the club was not always such a shining light among the football community, or that it's first taste of major success came even before the club found a place among the highest rank even of English football.

Indeed, when 'Spurs won the F.A. Challenge Cup for the first time in 1901 they were not even members of the Football League, then being members of the inferior Southern League, which, albeit, they had championed the season before. That victory represents the last ever occasion upon which a club from outside the Football League (and/or more latterly the Premier League) has won the national trophy.

What makes the achievement even more remarkable was that it ended nineteen years of Northern and Midlands domination during which time only one other Southern club (Southampton in 1900) had even reached the final. More than that even, after 'Spurs victory in 1901, it would be a further twenty years before the cup again found a resting place in the South – when the 'Spurs themselves won it for a second time in 1921!

This is the story of that first Cup campaign, told through the period press with additional facts and commentary by the author.

All football action line drawings reproduced in this book have been taken from various period issues of "Athletic News" (some may have been altered from their original form).

All advertisements from period press.

Illustrated Catalogue of 100 Varieties Post Free.

Mappin & Webb's LTD.
Chairman, J. NEWTON MAPPIN.

Illustrated Catalogue of 100 Varieties Post Free.

FITTED SUIT CASES FOR LADIES & GENTLEMEN.

BAGS MADE TO TAKE CUSTOMERS OWN FITTINGS.

ONLY LONDON ADDRESSES,
158 to 162, OXFORD ST., W., & 2, QUEEN VICTORIA ST., E.C.
SHEFFIELD—The Royal Works.   MANCHESTER—St. Ann's Square.   NICE—Place Jardin Public.   JOHANNESBURG—8, Von Brandis Square.   (Facing the Mansion House.)

REGISTERED TRADE MARK

HUNTING.
HAMMOND & CO., LTD.
(Established nearly a Century).
Leather Breeches and Trousers Makers, Military and Sporting Tailors,
465, OXFORD STREET, LONDON.

Branches:—Paris: 8, Place Vendôme, Brussels: 41, Boulevard de Waterloo; Newmarket; Cape Town, 40, Strand Street.   BY SPECIAL APPOINTMENT to
Telegraphic Addresses—"BREECHES."   LONDON, PARIS, BRUSSELS, NEWMARKET, CAPE TOWN.   HER LATE MAJESTY THE QUEEN, H.R.H. THE PRINCE OF WALES, H.I. & A.M. THE EMPEROR OF AUSTRIA, H.M. THE KING OF SPAIN, &c.

MOUNTED INFANTRY.
Knickerbocker Riding and Walking Pantaloons.
Patented June 26, 1901.

The above represents the model uniform as introduced by us, and approved for the officers of the Mounted Infantry.

Messrs. HAMMOND & CO. beg to draw attention to their new patent Legging, the advantage over any other kind being that there are no buttons and no straps round the leg to rub against the saddle or stirrup leather.

The same strap that holds the Legging together also forms an attachment on to the Breeches. Besides their extremely smart appearance they are much easier to fasten or unfasten than any other legging yet introduced.

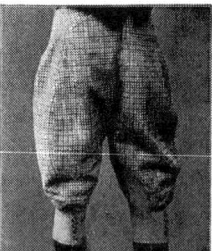

WARNING.
So-called Patent Knickerbockers or Riding Breeches without seam at the grip between knee and saddle.

Messrs. HAMMOND & CO. hereby give notice that they are the first inventors and makers of the above Breeches, and that all Patents for the same are invalid. The Court of Chancery has, on their petition, recently revoked two of these much-advertised Patents, and they will, after this notice, proceed against all persons claiming exclusive or patent rights in such garments.

Patterns and Forms for Self-Measurement sent on application.

THE HAMMOND LEGGING.
Patent No. 24,369.

Some Notes on Football in 1900/01

There were some significant differences in the way the Association game was played and organised during the period to which this publication relates, as compared to the current day. To enable readers to better understand the period match reports reproduced in this publication, let me first summarise the more significant of these differences, particularly with reference to any terms which may be used in these reports that are not so common in the current day.

Formation – The predominant playing formation of the era was 2-3-5, ie:
Outside Left – Inside Left – Centre Forward – Inside Right – Outside Right
(forwards)
Left Half – Centre Half - Right Half
(halves)
Left Back – Right Back
(backs)
Goalkeeper

Substitutes – match teams consisted of eleven players only, with **no** substitutes. Substitutes were not permitted in English League Football until the 1965-66 season. Prior to then, if a player was unable for any reason to continue to fully participate in the game then his team would have to play on a man short, or, in the case of the 'walking wounded', with the injured player switched to a less critical position - usually an outside wing where he would not compromise his teams defence and might still contribute to the attack with the occasional pass if the ball happened his way.

Players Kit – Players shirts bore neither numbers nor names for identification.

Goalkeepers – wore matching kit to the outfield players of the same team. Sometimes substituted a woollen jersey but this must be of the same colour. The rule requiring goalkeepers to wear distinctive tops (so they could be distinguished by referees in a melee of players) was introduced in 1909. Goalkeeper was a designation which could be switched to any other player at any time but only **after** informing the referee. could handle anywhere inside his own half but not carry.

Off-side – A player was off-side if there were less than **three** opponents between him and the opposing goal line at the moment when the ball was played forward to him by a member of his own side. The goalkeeper counted as, but needed not necessarily to be, one of the three. Player could be off-side in his own half of the field of play.

Floodlights – Although Floodlighting in association football dates as far back as 1878, when experimental floodlit matches were played at Bramall Lane, they did not become a regular part of the game until the 1950's. City's first floodlights were installed in 1954. Accordingly, before then, fixtures had to be timed to finish in daylight.

Match Ball – Match balls were made of stitched leather panels and were much heavier than modern footballs made of lightweight synthetic materials. Furthermore, in wet conditions a ball could more than double in weight due to the leather skin becoming waterlogged.

Divisions – The League was divided into only two divisions – First and Second. It was not until the 1920's that the League expanded – by adding two initially regional third divisions which later became nationalised as Divisions Three and Four.

Charging (a.k.a. Shoulder Charge) – A form of tackle wherein the tackler makes deliberate bodily contact with an opponent, leading with his shoulder against the opponents shoulder, in an effort to barge the opponent off the ball. This was/is legitimate so long as each player had/has one foot on the ground at the time of contact, and the amount of force used was/is not 'excessive'. Charging remains in the rules today, but the idea of what is regarded as excessive is now applied so stringently that the forceful charging of old has gone from the game.

£ s. d. - U.K. Pre-decimalisation currency: pounds (£ - librae), shillings (s - solidi) and pence (d - denarii) where £1 = 20s : 1s = 12d. Allowing for inflation, the sum of £1 in 1901 would be worth approximately the equivalent of £113 at 2017 prices[1].

Linesmen – the common term for referees assistants in the days before political correctness.

1   Source: http://inflation.stephenmorley.org.

The F.A. Challenge Cup

The current F.A. Challenge Cup trophy is actually the second of it's kind by design and the fifth by manufacture.

The First FA Cup

1. The first cup was used from 1872 to 1895 (stolen).
2. A duplicate copy of the first cup was manufactured and used from 1896 to 1910 (retired due to existence of unauthorised duplicate).
3. A new copyrighted design was introduced in 1911 and used until 1991 (retired due to wear and tear having caused the trophy to become fragile).
4. An exact duplicate was introduced in 1992 and used until 2013 (retired due to wear and tear).
5. Another but more sturdily constructed duplicate was introduced in 2014.

The origins of the F.A. Cup can be traced back to a meeting of the Football Association on July 20th, 1871, where it was proposed by C.W. Alcock, Secretary of the F.A., that a Challenge Cup be instituted for which all clubs belonging to the Association should be invited to compete. The proposal was approved unanimously and a committee constituted to draft the rules for the competition. Little could those present have realised that not only would their brainchild go on to become the pre-eminent sporting competition in England, it's concept would be copied across the entire globe.

Martin, Hall & Co. of Sheffield were then commissioned to create a trophy to be presented to the winners - the first cup being eighteen inches high and produced at a cost of £20.

The inaugural competition was something of an ad hoc affair, with just fifteen entrants most of which were based in the Greater London area, within moderate travelling distance of Kennington Oval where the final was to be contested. The major exceptions being Queens Park of Glasgow and Donington School of Lincolnshire. These two were drawn together, but when Donington 'scratched' Queens Park were given a bye to the semi-final stage. Three of the original applicants, Harrow Chequers, Reigate Priory and the afore-mentioned Donington School withdrew without playing a game, so that only twelve clubs actually contested the issue: Barnes, Civil Service, Clapham Rovers, Crystal Palace, Hampstead Heathens, Hitchin, Maidenhead, Marlow, Royal Engineers, The Wanderers, Upton Park and Queens Park. The first final was contested between the Wanderers and the Royal Engineers, with the former being the first winners.

Over the next few years the number of entrants to the competition grew, slowly at first, then in ever increasing numbers, and drawing in clubs from all over the country.

Initially, the Southern Public School and Old Boys clubs dominated the competition, but the advent of professionalism[2] into the game swung the balance firmly in favour of the working mens clubs of the North and Midlands. Blackburn Olympic were the first of the latter to capture the trophy in 1883, defeating the Old Etonians in the final. From that year onwards no Southern club again reached the final until Southampton in 1899, losing 0-4 to Bury.

Southampton, at the time, were reigning Southern League champions. A year later, Tottenham had wrested the Southern League championship from the South coast club and were looking to go one better than in the national Cup competition by securing the trophy for the South for the first time in 18 years.

FA Cup Winners 1872-1900

Year	Finalists	Entries[3]
1872	Wanderers 1 – Royal Engineers 0	15[4]
1873	Wanderers 2 – Oxford University 0	16
1874	Oxford University 2 – Royal Enginers 0	28
1875	Royal Engineers 2 – Old Etonians 1 (after 1-1 draw)	29
1876	Wanderers 3 – Old Etonians 1 (after 1-1 draw)	32
1877	Wanderers 2 – Oxford University 1	37
1878	Wanderers 3 – Royal Engineers 1	43
1879	Old Etonians 1 – Clapham Rovers 0	43
1880	Clapham Rovers 1 – Oxford University 0	54
1881	Old Carthusians 3 – Old Etonians 0	62
1882	Old Etonians 1 – Blackburn Rovers 0	73
1883	Blackburn Olympic 2 – Old Etonians 1	84
1884	Blackburn Rovers 2 – Queens Park 1	100
1885	Blackburn Rovers 2 – Queens Park 0	114
1886	Blackburn Rovers 2 – West Bromwich Albion 0 (after 0-0 draw)	130
1887	Aston Villa 2 – West Bromwich Albion 0	124
1888	West Bromwich Albion 2 – Preston North End 1	149
1889	Preston North End 3 – Wolverhampton Wanderers 0	32[5]
1890	Blackburn Rovers 6 – The Wednesday (Sheffield) 1	
1891	Blackburn Rovers 3 – Notts County 1	
1892	West Bromwich Albion 3 – Aston Villa 0	
1893	Wolverhampton Wanderers 1 – Everton 0	
1894	Notts County 4 – Bolton Wanderers 1	

---

2 The ban against professionalism was lifted in 1885, but even before then a form of clandestine professionalism was rife in the North and Midlands wherein players would be found jobs with sympathetic local businesses that paid above the average wage whilst allowing plenty of time off to play the game.
3 From wikipedia.
4 Three retired without playing.
5 Due to the number of clubs now entering a Qualifying tournament was introduced from which the last ten would henceforth join twenty-two seeded clubs in the Competition Proper.

1895   Aston Villa 1 – West Bromwich Albion 0
1896   The Wednesday (Sheffield) 2 – Wolverhampton Wanderers 1
1897   Aston Villa 3 – Everton 2
1898   Nottingham Forest 3 – Derby County 1
1899   Sheffield United 4 – Derby County 1
1900   Bury 4 – Southampton 0

'Spurs Cup History

1894/95 - *(Q1) v WEST HERTS 3-2; (Q2) v WOLVERTON 5-3; (Q3) at Clapton 4-1; (Q4) v LUTON 2-2, at Luton 0-4.*

1895/96 - *(Q1) at Luton Town 2-1; (Q2) at Vampires (Newbury) 0-4.*

1896/97 – *(Q1,Q2) bye; (Q3) v OLD St. STEPHENS 4-0; (Q4) v MAIDENHEAD 6-0; (Q5) at Luton 0-3.*

1897/98 – *(Q1,Q2) bye; (Q3) v 2nd COLDSTREAM GUARDS 7-0; (Q4) v LUTON 3-4.*

1898/99 – *(Q1,Q2) bye; (Q3) v WOLVERTON[6] 4-0; (Q4) v CLAPTON 2-1; (Q5) v LUTON 1-1, at Luton 2-0; (1P) v NEWTON HEATH 1-1, at Newton Heath 5-3; (2P) v SUNDERLAND 2-1; (QF) at Stoke 1-4.*

1899/00 - *Excused all qualifying rounds: (1P) at Preston North End 0-1.*

It seems quite extraordinary that in all five seasons in which 'Spurs played through the Qualifying rounds they at some point encountered Luton Town. It should be remembered, however, that the qualifying competition was regionalised, and that since 'Spurs and Luton were arguably the two best sides in their region involved in that stage of the competition, it was almost inevitable that it should fall upon one of them at some point to dismiss the other.

---

6   'Spurs purchased home rights for £50 + expenses.

English League v. Southern League

In the early years of English Football, apart from various regional cup competitions, there was no formal competition through which the various clubs could routinely fill up their annual fixture lists. Instead they faced an annual ritual of sending out and answering invitations to play in friendly or challenge matches, and dealing with the many cancellations such an informal system inevitably involved.

When professionalism was first permitted in the game from 1885 many of the clubs from the Northern and Midland industrial centres chose to follow this route. Many, indeed, were already professional to some degree (in all but name), and had collectively forced the F.A.'s hand in lifting the ban. With professionalism, however, came a substantial financial burden which meant that the old haphazard way of arranging fixtures was no longer adequate. Cricket had solved the fixture problem by the formation of 'leagues' whose members would play each other annually on an organised basis. Consequently, a dozen of the top English football clubs copied this example by joining together to form their own Football League with the same purpose.

The English League was founded in 1888, expanding to two divisions in 1892, with the intention of it's being a national organisation covering all parts of the country. It's twelve founder members all came from the industrial centres of the North and Midlands, however, where the professional game, at the time, had most strongly taken hold, and for a number of years (largely due to a continuing resistance to professionalism in the South) it remained an essentially Northern and Midlands organisation (in actuality if not intent). The first southern club to be admitted were Woolwich Arsenal in 1893.

By this time professionalism was beginning to take more of a hold in the South also, especially in London (the 'Spurs turned professional in 1895), and since the clubs there still lacked this level of organisation, in 1894, the Southern League was founded as a Southern equivalent of the Northern based English League. From it's sixteen initial members, the Southern League quickly expanded to dominate in the South and include all of the best Southern clubs. At it's height, whilst one or two of the better clubs in the South may have been of sufficient standard to have survived in the English League First Division, the general playing standard of the top Division in the Southern competition was probably around or slightly lower than that of the English League Second Division.

This was approximately the situation in 1901, with the 'Spurs being one of those better Southern clubs, indeed the current champions - having won the title for the first time the previous season, putting them probably about on a par with the better Division Two clubs. Their Cup Final opponents, Sheffield United, on the other hand, were the regnant runners-up to the English League First Division title, though currently enduring a more mediocre season.

A Short History of Tottenham Hotspur F.C.

Whilst Tottenham Hotspur could be classed among the pioneers of the professional game in the South of England, in the wider scheme of the game as a whole they were, at the time, relative upstarts, having been formed as an amateur organisation[7] in 1882, some ten years after the Wanderers won the first F.A. Cup tournament! But if they were not then to be counted among the earliest of Southern clubs, they quickly rose from humble beginnings to be counted among the finest.

Like so many others, the football club arose as an adjunct to a cricket club – in this case the Hotspur Cricket Club, which was itself still in it's infancy, having been established only two years earlier. The Cricket club had been formed by schoolboys primarily from the St. John's Middle Class School in Tottenham and the Tottenham Grammar School. It's members, and those of the football club, were initially drawn from pupils of those and several other boarding schools in the area.

The name 'Hotspur' was derived from the Northumberland family, local landowners who, indeed, owned the land on which the cricket club played it's home fixtures. A famous figure in the ancestral line of the Northumberlands was Sir Henry Percy, better known as 'Harry Hotspur', or simply 'Hotspur' – a name bestowed on him by the Scots for his hot-blooded urgency and readiness to attack at every opportunity whilst supporting King Richard II of England against them during the Anglo-Scottish wars.

Early football matches were played on public land at the Northern end of Tottenham Marshes, which lie between the railway line and the river Lea, and despite playing against generally older sides the boys did well and soon attracted a following. Playing on public land, however, the club could not charge admission. As their reputation continued to grow, in 1885 'Tottenham' was added to the club name to avert growing confusion with the similarly named London Hotspurs club.

It soon became obvious that the club needed a ground of it's own, where they could welcome paying spectators if progress was to be maintained, and a search was begun to find a suitable location. The result was a field just across the railway lines at Northumberland Park, and having obtained it's lease the club moved in for the start of the 1888/89 season. One of the early visitors there were the legendary Old Etonians in a tie for the London Senior Cup. 'Spurs closely matched the veteran cup fighters in the first half, going into the interval with only a one goal deficit at 2-3. When the Etonians released their full potential in the second half, however, 'Spurs were overwhelmed, conceding five more goals without reply.

With a venue of their own, the club advanced from strength to strength. In 1893 'Spurs applied to be included among those clubs that founded the Southern League but were rejected on that occasion. Undeterred, the club went about raising it's profile and in 1894 the first stand was built on the Northumberland Park ground, providing just 100 seats with changing rooms beneath. In 1895 the club turned professional and the

---

7   At that time all clubs were amateur since professionalism was banned in the game.

following year were successful in gaining acceptance into the ranks of the Southern League (then in it's third season).

By now, however, increasing crowds were already beginning to tax the capacity of the Northumberland Park ground, and before long the club were looking for a new venue with greater potential. In 1899, the answer was found in a site known as Beckwith's Nursery, a former plant nursery, now fallen into disuse, owned by the Charringtons brewing company and located behind the White Hart public house off the high road at Tottenham. A twenty-one lease was secured from the owners, whereupon work began in preparing the site for football.

A New Ground

Throughout the summer months of 1899 gangs of working men were kept well employed in making the new site ready for football. The greenhouses were demolished and the debris removed, following which a pitch was laid out fully 118 by 80 yards in dimension, with a further five yards separating the touchlines from the white picket fence that held back the crowd. Terraces were raised on three sides of the playing area, whilst on the fourth was re-erected the old stand from the former ground flanked by two huge new structures. The old stand, which held 400 persons, was reserved for shareholders in the company, whilst the two new stands, each capable of holding 900 persons, raised the overall seating capacity to 2,200 (1,800 more than Northumberland Park). Beneath one of the new stands were incorporated spacious and well-appointed dressing-rooms for the teams whilst the other contained a commodious refreshments area with a serving bar one hundred feet long. The result was one of the largest and finest grounds in the whole of the South of England.

For all it's benefits and advantages, however, the new ground, at the time of it's opening, had one serious flaw - the only portals for egress being on the pub side of the ground, creating a potentially dangerous bottleneck for supporters exiting after a game. The reason for this was contained in the terms for the lease that the 'Spurs had signed with Charringtons, and which required all visitors to pass their 'house' when attending the venue. Despite this defect, the new ground was officially opened on 5th September, 1899, with a friendly match against First Division Notts. County.

04/09/1899 - TOTTENHAM HOTSPURS v. NOTTS COUNTY
Sporting Life - Tuesday 5th September, 1899
AN EASY WIN FOR THE SPURS.

Few grounds in the neighbourhood of London can compare with the new enclosure of the Tottenham Hotspur F.C. at White Hart Lane. Yesterday evening the Notts County Team played a friendly game with the Spurs in the presence of a crowd numbering between 6,000 and 7,000. The visitors were not so strongly represented as they were on Saturday, when they defeated last year's runners-up for the F.A. Cup. Lowe came in at half-back in place of Calderhead, while Cairns was in McMain's place in the centre. The play was fairly even during the first half, but the home team failed make the most of their opportunities. Time and again the goal was at their mercy, but the shooting was distinctly faulty. Cameron seems to have lost a lot of his dash and gained a good deal of weight. Tait made a favourable impression in Cain's place, and Smith showed pace and cleverness on the outside right. The Notts team were the cleverer, and showed capital combination at this early period of the season. Bull was the pick of the back division, and Suter was very safe in goal. McNaught was very clever, and kept his team well together, more particularly in the second half, when he was very much all there.

During the first few minutes the Spurs pressed, but subsequently Hadley, on the left, broke away, and the ball went behind. Cameron led a smart attack, and, following some capital passing by the whole of the forwards, Kirwan shot, but Suter saved at the cost of being floored. The game was delayed for some moments to enable the Notts custodian time to recover. As soon as play was resumed Suter was called upon to use his hands twice in quick succession. Chalmers was responsible for a clever run, but Tait hampered him when the final shot was about to be taken, and as a result the ball went behind. Both sides displayed plenty of cleverness, each were in turn dangerous. Half an hour from the commencement the Notts carried the ball well into the home territory, and Clawley only met a shot in moderate fashion. McCairns regained possession, and promptly sent on to Fletcher, the latter passed to Chalmers, who in turn, centred to McCairns, and with a clinking shot the latter scored. When a restart was made, Tait was responsible for some clever work: this relieved the pressure which the Midlanders were forcing. The game was carried to the opposite end, where two poor shots were made at the visitors' citadel. Kirwan, who was continually doing good work, cleverly gained a corner through sending the leather on to an opposing back at a time when an attempt to shoot would have been useless. Of some fast play the homesters were seen to the best advantage, and after they had twice sent behind, Cameron sent in a low swift shot from which Suter made a magnificent save. Some clever passing ensued between the home forwards, and after each of the front rank had engaged in some passing, Kirwan centred to **Pratt**, who with a hard shot equalised. From now until the interval the exchanges were of an even character, and when the teams crossed over, the score stood: Hotspur, one goal; Notts, one goal.

When the game resumed Jones and Morris changed positions. The homesters soon became the aggressors, but the ball was forced behind. From the goal-kick the Notts left wing broke away, and Clawley ran out a considerable distance to meet a shot made by Maconnachie. This enabled the Spurs to again assume the offensive, and after Cameron hit the upright with a hard shot, Copeland sent behind. The visitors were compelled to act on the defensive until Lewis relieved, and then by some clever movements the Midlander's front rank carried the venue of the game to the other end. The ball travelled into the respective divisions with marked rapidity, and Tait called forth loud applause by his superb play. The old Prestonian completely nonplussed Hadley at a moment when the last named threatened danger. Cameron, after a fine single-handed run, misjudged his pace, which assisted the opposing custodian to negotiate an otherwise dangerous intrusion. Two corners fell to the Spurs in quick succession, and for some moments they pressed severely. Smith, the wing, was conspicuous for a couple of smart runs. Still maintaining the pressure, the locals gained some assistance through Montgomery miss-kicking, and with the forwards busy **Pratt** was afforded opportunity to score, an opening he utilised, to the delight of the local supporters. Having taken the lead the Spurs appeared determined to retain their advantage, and continued to keep the Midlanders on the defence. Cameron made two very feeble shots with the goal at his mercy, and immediately after Suter in turning aside a high shot was badly charged, and had to retire. Bull, who took up his position between the sticks, soon proved his efficiency, as within his first five minutes in that position he made four capital saves. A combined rush by the visitors was evaded by McNaught, who retains all his old skill. Smith in a long dribble outpaced Montgomery and the centre of the former brought about a melee in the goal mouth. Bull found useful assistance from the backs in averting. McNaught prevented a rush made at his end, and Morris obtaining possession sent on to Cameron, against whom off-side was reasonably claimed. With no official announcement to stop, the home forwards continued to make headway, and Copeland sent the leather into the net after colliding heavily with the custodian. The visitors were dismayed at their appeal not being acknowledged, and with the exception of Bull, made no attempt to stop the progress of their opponents. The Spurs clearly demonstrated superiority at this stage, and after Cameron's shot into the net was nullified through a claim for off-side, Copeland added a fourth point for the Spurs. Nothing more was obtained by either side during the remaining ten minutes, and when the whistle sounded Notts retired vanquished by an unexpected majority.

RESULT: TOTTENHAM HOTSPUR 2 – NOTTS. COUNTY 1

TOTTENHAM: Clawley (goal); Erentz and Tait (backs); Jones, McNaught and Morris (halves); Smith, Pratt [2], Copeland, Carmeron and Kirwan (forwards).
NOTTS Co.: Suter (goal); Lewis and Montgomery (backs); Ball, Bull and Lowe (halves); Hadley, Maconnachie, McCairns [1], Fletcher and Chalmers (forwards).
Referee: Mr. C.D. Crisp.

'Spurs bought the freehold for the White Hart Lane ground in 1905, freeing them from the restrictions of the lease they had entered into with Charringtons. Following the purchase the ground was substantially redeveloped, addressing the access problems.

Note that during the period covered by this book the 'Spurs played in plain white shirts with no badge, and navy blue knickers[8]. The now familiar cockerel shirt badge was not implemented until 1921.

---

8   Prior to the adoption of this iconic combination several others had been experimented with, including: white and sky blue halves, blue and white stripes, red shirts over blue knickers and even chocolate and gold stripes over blue knickersl.

Southern League Champions

The 1899/1900 season began with Southampton as hot favourites to win their fourth successive Southern League title. 'Spurs, meanwhile, were looking to recover from the poor showing of the previous season which had seen them finish half-way down the table, but were buoyed up at the prospect of their first season in their new White Hart Lane ground. Indeed 'Spurs got off to a magnificent start, winning eleven of their first thirteen Southern League encounters. With Southampton living up to expectations, and Portsmouth also on top form, by the turn of the millennium, with the season at it's midway point, it was already looking like a three-horse race. Southampton led the way with 25 points from 15 games, followed by 'Spurs on 21 points and Portsmouth on 19, both from 13 games. With two points awarded for a win, 'Spurs games in hand had the potential to draw them level so it could hardly have been closer. Bristol City lagged only a further two points behind Portsmouth but had played three more games.

As Easter approached the teams had switched positions but remained in equally close contention. Southampton had now slipped to third, mainly due to missed games which remained to be rearranged. In a 28 game season, 'Spurs now led the way on 38 points from 24 games played, followed by Portsmouth on 35 from 24, and Southampton on 31 from 21 (with a potential to reach 37 points from their games in hand). By now the breakaway of this group was complete, the next club, Reading, being mathematically out of range of making any impression on the leaders in the games remaining.

Consequently, Easter arrived with a tight schedule of fixtures that looked certain to have a heavy impact on the destination of that year's Southern League title. These included Southampton facing off against both their rivals, a tough proposition for the south coast club but also a perfect opportunity to take back control of the title race.

Southampton, however, had also reached the final of the F.A. Challenge Cup, due to be played the following weekend, and, perhaps distracted by this, began the Easter programme badly, wasting one of their games in hand to a shock 4-1 reverse at struggling Thames Ironworks (now West Ham United). Consequently, the import of 'the big one', 'Spurs v Southampton at White Hart Lane on Good Friday, was raised even higher. It was now a must win game for the Saints to stop 'Spurs pulling clear and leave their own hopes alive.

13/04/1900 - TOTTENHAM HOTSPUR v. SOUTHAMPTON
The Sportsman - Saturday 14th April, 1900
THE SOTIONIANS VIRTUALLY LOSE THE CHAMPIONSHIP

By their defeat yesterday at Tottenham, Southampton practically surrendered their chance of retaining the above championship, which had been reduced to a minimum at Canning Town last Monday. On Boxing Day they had been successful at home by three goals to one, but the 'Spurs now avenged that reverse by scoring twice without response. Favoured with a fine afternoon, there was an enormous attendance - just under fifteen thousand - with a gate of £866, which constitutes a record for the competition. Both placed full strength in the field, except that for the visitors MacLeod played centre forward instead of Farrell. A high wind prevailed, but it scarcely interfered with the game to the extent anticipated. Facing both it and the sun for the first half, the 'Spurs nevertheless scored at the end of the first eight minutes, Meehan missing an attempt to clear, and **Cameron** landing the ball into the net. Prior to this, however, Chadwick had put in a splendid ground shot, which Haddow manage to save at the expense of a corner. The home team subsequently held the upper hand, and once Robinson riskily ran out to save, while on another occasion he had to throw away. Towards the interval, however, the balance certainly lay with the Sotonian's, but their shooting was erratic. Millward sent over the bar from a long shot by Meehan, Yates lost a good chance by sending wide, and Chadwick twice had hard luck, once hitting the bar with a splendid shot from long range, and directly after kicking just too high. Thus, at half-time the 'Spurs still led by a goal to love.

Southampton in the first few minutes of the second stage pressed strongly, but from a free kick well placed by Tait, **Cameron** again put the ball into the net six minutes from the restart by a clever piece of footwork. This virtually settled matters, and though occasionally the visiting forwards broke away, it cannot be said that they were as dangerous as usual. Nor could the 'Spurs, though doing most of the attacking, increase their advantage, though Pratt put through when offside, the referee allowing a free kick for a previous foul - a ruling which evidently disturbed the equanimity[9] of the visiting goalkeeper. Nothing accrued, Robinson also cleverly clearing a fine shot from Copeland, and Tottenham left the field victors by two goals to love, having played the better football. It cannot be claimed, however, that the game was a great one, there being plenty of good individual play, but a lack of combination.

RESULT: TOTTENHAM HOTSPUR 2 – SOUTHAMPTON 0

TOTTENHAM: Haddow (goal); Melia and Tait (backs); Morris, McNaught and Stormont (halves); Smith, Cameron [2], Pratt, Copeland and Kirwan (forwards).
SOUTHAMPTON: Robinson (goal); Meehan and Durber (backs); Newton, Chadwick and Petrie (halves); Turner, Yates, McLeod, Wood and Millward (forwards).
Referee: Mr. F.H. King.

The following day (Saturday) 'Spurs uncharacteristically lost (0-3) at Bristol City, but any slight glimmer of hope that defeat might otherwise have brought to Southampton was nullified by their own further 2-0 defeat on the same day at home to Portsmouth. Worse, on Easter Monday, Southampton lost to Portsmouth again by the same margin in the return fixture at Fratton Park whilst on the same day the 'Spurs' defeated Sheppey United at White Hart Lane – the latter game being interrupted for several minutes by an unseasonally severe hailstorm that caused the players to rush for cover. Four defeats in as many days brought the Saints hopes of retaining their Southern League title to an emphatic end, and worse for them was yet to come – their sudden loss of true form continued into the Cup final where they failed to give a true account of

---

9   The Saints keeper, Robinson, was later suspended for two weeks, to be served at the commencement of the following season, for misconduct during the match.

themselves against an albeit powerful English League First Division outfit in Bury, succumbing to a 4-0 defeat, and thus ending their season in crushing anti-climax.

Portsmouth, on the other hand, as well as eliminating Southampton from the title race altogether had also cut 'Spurs five point lead over themselves to just three – but with two games left to them to play against 'Spurs one. 'Spurs had no game the following Saturday (Cup Final Day) allowing Portsmouth to increase the pressure and reduce the gap to a single point by despatching Millwall 2-0 in a rearranged fixture. Consequently, with one game remaining, the title was 'Spurs to lose, a victory would ensure them success, but any slip would surely find Portsmouth waiting.

28/04/1900 – NEW BROMPTON v. TOTTENHAM HOTSPUR
The Sportsman - Monday 30th April, 1900
NEW BROMPTON v. TOTTENHAM HOTSPUR
THE SPURS WIN THE CHAMPIONSHIP

The match between these clubs at New Brompton on Saturday, was of prime importance to the 'Spurs, for if they lost there was the possibility of Portsmouth's being returned as Champions of the League. The Londoners, however, were found on the winning side, and they are to be congratulated upon their success, which, it must be admitted by all who take an interest in Southern football, has been well earned. New Brompton invariably prove awkward customers to meet on their own ground, and Tottenham's victory by two goals to one was only gained after a stoutly contested game. In fact the game was in doubt until close on the finish, and on the run of the play there was not much to choose between the two teams. Fine weather prevailed, and the spectators numbered about 3000, including a strong contingent from Tottenham, who "chaired" the winners at the close of the game. The visitors won the toss, and made the home side face the sun. There was hardly any breeze, and both teams at once settled down to their work. Forcing the pace, the 'Spurs initiated several warm attacks, and Carter was quickly engaged in repelling shots from Cameron, Kirwan, and Pratt, whilst the last named failed to take advantage of a fairly easy chance. The Brompton forwards then got together, and after Clawley had cleared from Swan, he was beaten with a grounder from **Gladwell**, greatly to the delight of the local partisans. For the remainder of the first half the play certainly favoured the home side, and from a pass by Swan, Grey netted the ball, but after consulting the linesman the referee disallowed the point for offside. At the interval Brompton led by a goal to love.

On resuming, the visitors went for all they were worth, and at once forced two unfruitful corners. Three minutes, however, had only elapsed when **Cameron**, receiving from Morris, scored with a shot which appeared to deceive the custodian, who made no attempt to catch the ball. For some minutes the home defence was hard pressed, but the 'Spurs found it impossible to augment their total. A bad pass by Frettingham spoiled a promising attack, and Clawley saved from Innes and the centre man. Ten minutes from the close the 'Spurs made a big effort, and although Carter got a drive from McNaught, he was beaten by a header from **Copeland**, an appeal that the custodian had been impeded being overruled. Nothing further was scored and the visitors won as stated.

RESULT: TOTTENHAM HOTSPUR 2 – NEW BROMPTON 1

TOTTENHAM: Clawley (goal); Erentz and Tait (backs); McNaught, Jones and Morris (halves); Smith, Cameron [1], Pratt, Copeland [1] and Kirwan (forwards).
NEW BROMPTON: Carter (goal); Robertson and Glover (backs); Innes, Atherton and Graham (halves); Gladwell [1], T. Gray, Frettingham, Swan and Sealey (forwards).
Referee: Mr. Muir.

'Spurs victory rendered Portsmouth's remaining game, the following Monday, irrelevant, and secured the club's first senior championship title. A result made all the more meritorious by the closeness of the chase and the calibre of the opposition.

SOUTHERN LEAGUE – Final Table

Division One 1899/1900   HOME

	Pld	W	D	L	F	A	Avg	Pts
Tottenham Hotspur	28	20	4	4	67	26	2.58	**44**
Portsmouth	28	20	1	7	59	29	2.03	**41**
Southampton	28	17	1	10	70	33	2.12	**35**
Reading	28	15	2	11	41	28	1.46	**32**
Swindon Town	28	15	2	11	50	42	1.19	**32**
Bedminster	28	13	2	13	44	45	0.98	**28**
Millwall Athletic	28	12	3	13	36	37	0.97	**27**
Queens Park Rangers	28	12	2	14	50	58	0.86	**26**
Bristol City	28	9	7	12	44	47	0.94	**25**
Bristol Rovers	28	11	3	14	46	55	0.84	**25**
New Brompton	28	9	6	13	39	49	0.80	**24**
Gravesend United	28	10	4	14	38	58	0.66	**24**
Chatham Town	28	10	3	15	38	58	0.66	**23**
Thames Ironworks	28	8	5	15	30	45	0.67	**21**
Sheppey United	28	3	7	18	24	66	0.36	**13**
Brighton United	0	0	0	0	0	0	0.00	**0**
Cowes	0	0	0	0	0	0	0.00	**0**

Brighton Utd retired mid season - 22 matches, record expunged.

Cowes retired mid season – 13 matches, record expunged.

The bottom two clubs in the First Division met top two of Second Division in promotion/relegation play-off matches: Thames Ironworks (now West Ham United) beat Fulham 5-1 to retain their place; Sheppey United lost 1-2 to Watford who replaced them in the top flight.

Consequently, 'Spurs embarked upon the 1900/01 season as defending Southern League champions, but whilst they remained largely supreme at White Hart Lane poor away form kept them from mounting a serious challenge to repeat the Success. Unlike

Southampton the previous year, by the time the Cup came around in early February, there was little impediment towards devoting their fullest attention to that competition.

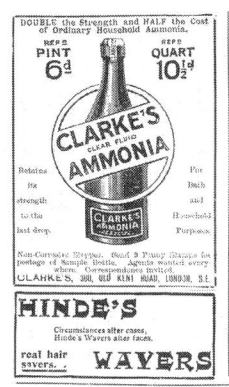

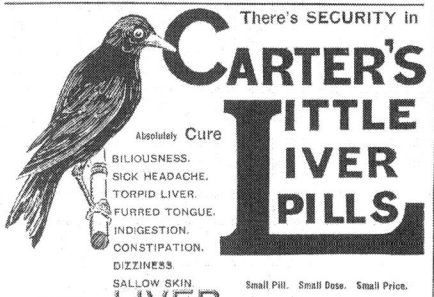

The Climate of the Time

At the start of the 1900/01 season English, indeed British, football was in the doldrums. During the 1899/1900 season there had been a general apathy among the general public towards the game and this had been reflected in the performances of the players. Crowds had, for most of the season, been significantly reduced from the previous season's levels, and with spirited partisanship largely absent from the grounds the football served up had, generally, been equally uninspiring.

Consequently takings were down and only a handful of the better supported clubs had been able to show a profit on the season, whilst others had been forced to struggle to make ends meet on greatly reduced incomes - especially those clubs in the North. Everton, for example, despite improving their League ranking from 11th to 7th, saw their total receipts fall from over £10,000 to only just over £7,500.

The reason for this was that Great Britain was, at the time, at War! Moreover, she was fighting a war that she thought she had already won! In 1880, British attempts to annexe the Transvaal in South Africa had met with resistance from the Dutch colonists, the Trekboers, leading to the First Boer War (December 1880 – March 1881). It was a short but bloody conflict ending in a treaty by which the Boers were granted self-government but under British suzerainty. It was an uneasy peace, however, and war broke out again in October 1899, with the Boers this time being much better prepared, and winning several important early battles against the overconfident and ill-prepared British. Consequently, back in Great Britain, reservists were hurriedly called up (there was no general conscription) and thousands of additional troops sent out to the continent to begin the fight back.

All of this had had a profound effect on the mood at home, where the news in the early months of the new conflict had been nearly all bad. With thousands of men gone away to fight, and public attention focused on the conflict, interest in football had waned considerably, and it was not until the following summer, by which time the pendulum of war had begun to swing toward the British interests that the situation began to change significantly. The arrival of British forces to break the siege of Mafeking in May 1900, for example, was a huge national relief - at last restoring public confidence in a positive outcome.

Consequently, the 1900/01 season began with football matters showing strong signs of recovery, and the fans returning in increasing numbers, so that, by Christmas, the pre-war status quo had largely been restored. This recovery was then somewhat disturbed, however, by the death, on 22nd January, 1901, of the Nation's beloved monarch, Queen Victoria. Competitive football was virtually suspended for a period of around three weeks whist the country was in mourning, throwing the remaining part of the fixture schedule into chaos.

An International Interlude

An interesting spectacle was seen at White Hart Lane shortly before the rounds of Cup ties began with the visit of a Berlin XI. Football in Germany was then still very much in it's infancy, it's further development being hampered by a negative image of the game resulting from the generally poor international relations that then existed between Britain and Germany (largely due to Germany's Imperial ambitions constantly bumping up against Britain's existing empire). Consequently, since football was generally regarded in Germany as being a quintessentially British eccentricity, it was commonly held in the same general level of contempt as afternoon tea parties and the famous British stiff upper lip – the Germans preferring instead to largely focus their sporting inclinations on the more serious business of athletics.

Still, there were several clubs in the German Capital, Berlin, who had formed their own F.A. and were seeking to make progress in developing the level of football there. This, they felt, could best be done by learning the English methods as they were practised on English grounds by the best English clubs. Consequently the Berlin F.A. had arranged for a representative XI to conduct a short tour of (mostly) Southern England playing against the better Southern Sides .

Spurs (hoops) v Berliners

The third game in the series of six was against 'Spurs at White Hart Lane on 8th January, 1901, the game being played on a pitch that was inches deep in snow. Due to the weather conditions only 800 spectators turned out to watch the game. 'Spurs ran up an easy five goal lead by half time then switched their eleven around for the second half to try the players in unaccustomed positions. The result was a more even second half, with 'Spurs still winning overall by nine goals to six.

The results of the tour were as follows (Germans score first):
5th Jan, 1901 – at Southampton 1-5
7th Jan, 1901 – at Aston Villa 2-6
8th Jan, 1901 – at Tottenham 6-9
10th Jan, 1901 – at Millwall 2-8
14th Jan, 1901 – v Richmond at Crystal Palace 1-7

F.A. CUP - FIRST ROUND

From the original 15 entrants in 1871, the number 30 years later had grown to 215. Of these, 22 seeded clubs were advanced to the First Round Proper, whilst the remainder were required to fight through several preliminary rounds in a qualifying competition to earn one of the 10 remaining places. The seeds that year were made up of the previous year's four semi-finalists, the seventeen other highest ranked clubs in the English League (which included First Division runners-up Sheffield United), and the Champions of the Southern League (Tottenham Hotspur). It was Spur's fourth appearance in the First Round Proper, a record for the Southern League shared only by Kettering (who were new to the League that year). By chance, Tottenham were drawn against the same opponents as the previous year – Lancastrians, Preston North End.

In the last quarter of the 19th Century the North and Midlands, and especially Lancashire, had been the powerhouse of English football, and the birthplace of professionalism in the game. After the passing of the Factories Act of 1850, which shut down the factories at noon on Saturdays and gave the workers an afternoon of leisure, countless football clubs had been formed to take advantage of this free time. Many of these working men's clubs were directly connected with the factories and/or supported by the wealthy owners who took an interest in the game. The game at the time was strictly amateur but it became common in the North for the best players to be found jobs in the mills and factories that not only paid unusually well but allowed plenty of time off to practice football. The Northern "shamateurs" soon outstripped the southern amateurs in terms of organisation and tactics and forced the F.A., in 1885, to recognise professional as part of the game – although it would take some time further for it to become widespread in the South. It was in this climate that Preston North End had risen to greatness, producing a side that had won the first two Football League championships, on the first occasion winning the F.A. Cup that year also. Then they had been known as 'The Invincibles', carrying all before them.

But things had changed since then, whilst the Northern sides still largely held sway over their Southern counterparts, Lancashire had lost it's particular dominance in that area and Preston in particular had spent the last few years falling ever closer to the foot of the First Division table. Still they had a strong side, capable of giving a good account of themselves in a cup tie. Certainly they had done that the year before, winning a battle royale in a cup tie against the Spurs at Deepdale. Now they were drawn against each other again.

On this occasion the 'Spurs, the Southern League title holders, had been playing well in the weeks leading up to the match whilst North End faced an unenviable struggle near the foot of the English League Division One table. Snow had fallen heavily in mid-week but the ground had been fully cleared and the pitch was in good condition, if a bit slippery on the surface. The Prestonians had come to town on Friday so as to be fully fit and rested for the match. For the benefit of the team, the Midland Railway had added a dining car to the train to enable them to dine in style on the journey. Centre-forward, Thomas Pratt, for the Prestonians was an ex-Tottenham man.

Like Preston, Sheffield United were having a tough time of it in the League that season, and their own cup draw saw them facing a trip to Sunderland to meet one of the leading First Division Championship contenders. Given their difference in League form and standing, and with the added benefit of home advantage, Sunderland were the favourites for the tie.

The ties were scheduled to be played on Saturday 26th January, 1901, but following the death of Her Majesty Queen Victoria a few days earlier, on January 22nd, the Emergency Committee of the F.A. had decreed that all cup ties be suspended from that date in deference to the state of national morning then extant over Her Majesty's passing. The ties were postponed to February 9th, the date initially set for the second round. The ban related to the Cup competition only, however, and Tottenham took advantage of the now free Saturday to settle their outstanding Southern League fixture with Bristol Rovers which had been postponed earlier in the season. Two goals in each half without reply provided a perfect fillip to their cup ambitions.

There was much debate at the time as to the potential use of Spurs White Hart Lane ground to host the 12th staging of the annual North v. South match, to be played on Monday, 25th February. Crystal Palace had become by now the usual venue for major games played in the capital but had proven particularly unsuitable for supporters travelling from the North. Their trains usually disgorged at Kings Cross leaving the fans with a nine mile journey across the Thames and into South London to accomplish in order to reach the venue – many of them often arriving well after kick-off. White Hart Lane, on the other hand, was well appointed, and sited in North London, closer to and more easily reachable from Kings Cross as well as having links of it's own to the Northern network. Moreover, a successful staging of the match could have established the ground's potential as a future venue for cup finals! In the event, however, the F.A. chose to remain true to Crystal Palace.

TOTTENHAM HOTSPUR v. PRESTON NORTH END
First Round Proper – Saturday 9th February, 1901
Athletic News - Monday 11th February, 1901
GREAT BATTLE AT TOTTENHAM
[By Citizen]

The curious coincidence which brought Tottenham Hotspur and Preston North End together again in the first round of the Association Cup has already been dealt with. Last year a great fight was fought at Deepdale, and the result was a victory for Preston, rather a lucky victory, too, as the Prestonians were ready to admit at the close. On that day I saw McBride keep goal for the first time, and his performance ranks in my Memory with anything I have ever seen. Saturday saw the venue changed. Preston came up to Tottenham, and from the very start were assured of a trying time. Neither side has done too well in League matches this season, but Tottenham enthusiasts were able to congratulate themselves on the fact that their men had at last come back to last year's form. There was a great crowd on the ground, and although no official figures were forthcoming, 20,000 would be about the number present. It was certainly a record gate. It was soon seen that the ground was in a terribly heavy condition, snow and thaw on top of the frost making it sticky and holding. Instead of this suiting the "Spurs" as it usually does, the Prestonians seemed to like it best. For ten minutes or so, North End were on top. Shots were rained in upon Clawley from all quarters, and but for his coolness at a very critical period Tottenham might have experienced a veritable debacle. The fever wore of, however, and then the fun began.

A CONTRAST IN STYLE

The weakness which has characterised the Tottenham play almost throughout the season, was, however, very much apparent to the spectators. The three inside men were slow, and when they did get the ball, dallied in front of goal, waiting for impossible openings which never came. When a good chance did present itself they were time and again charged off the ball. Not the Preston men. Their passing was good, but they did not attempt to overdo it in front of goal. Shots, often badly directed it is true, were aimed at the Hotspur citadel, and many a gasp went round the ground as one effort better directed than its fellows just skimmed over the bar or went wide of the posts. Kirwan and Smith, the Tottenham wing men, however, could not be accused of any dalliance. Speedy, tricky, valiant, they both fought out every yard with their opponents. Curiously enough, it was the three inside men who impressed the most on the Preston side. Pratt we know well in the South, and he played the game he has so often played for the 'Spurs. Charging through the mud he seemed to endeavour to force his way through by sheer weight and pluck. He met his match, however, in Tait and Erentz, who never faltered, although for a time they were sorely beset, and often in desperate corners.

A WEAK HALF

There was one weak spot in the Tottenham half-back line. Morris has been playing forward all the year, and he has acquired the forward's habit of letting the man go when beaten. This was frequently dangerous, as Becton was at his best and working hard, harder than I have ever seen him work, and gave Mr. Morris a bad time occasionally. The only goal of the first half was scored from a corner for Preston. Green took the kick, and placed it very wide. One of the Hotspur players got his foot to the ball and sent it up the field to McMahon. Without waiting the young Preston back tried his hand at a long shot, and it came off. Clawley, hampered by a crowd of players, never saw the ball until too late, and it skimmed through the goal. This was just half an hour from the start, and it was a well deserved point. After this Tottenham played up desperately, and McBride made some grand saves. Kirwan and Smith troubled him the most, but he was not to be beaten, although the ball on one occasion touched his outstretched hand, and then the post, falling just in front of goal. He fell on it just as two or three of the Hotspur forwards dashed up, and in a scene of great excitement got it away. There were several similar incidents in front of both goals.

In the second half Tottenham attacked strenuously, and seemed to do everything but score. Try as they would, they could never get past the impassable McBride. Kirwan and Smith kept pegging away with their centres, but all to no purpose.

A LATE EQUALISER

At last, just before the close, Kirwan got away splendidly on the Tottenham left. He sent the ball right across the Preston goal. **Brown** flung himself at it, touched it with his head, and hey presto! it was through. There was a tremendous scene, hats, sticks, umbrellas went up, and the shouting lasted for fully a minute. Brown had shortly before missed an open goal, so his success was the more welcome to him. Teams were both at full strength.

RESULT: TOTTENHAM HOTSPUR 1 – PRESTON NORTH END 1

TOTTENHAM: Clawley (goal); Erentz and Tait (backs); Morris, McNaught and Stormont (halves); Smith, Cameron, Brown [1], Copeland and Kirwan (forwards).
NORTH END: McBride (goal); Dunn and McMahon [1] (backs); Elliott, McIntyre and Tod (halves); Parker, Gara, Pratt, Becton and Green (forwards).
Referee: Mr. A. G. Hines (Nottingham).

Most reports of the match agree that it was only the sterling work of McBride in goal that saved the Prestonians from certain defeat. Tottenham's centre-half McNaught suffered an injury to the ribs early in the game but played to the end, although at considerably below his best. The replay was set for the following Wednesday. Tottenham travelled North on the Monday to stay at the Royal Hotel, Southport, and prepare for the match in the fresh sea air.

PRESTON NORTH END v. TOTTENHAM HOTSPUR
First Round, Replay – Wednesday 13th February, 1901
The Sportsman - Thursday 14th February, 1901

These teams met at Preston yesterday to decide their drawn game in the Cup ties. The weather was fine and frosty, and the ground in perfect order, the sun having thawed the surface. The 'Spurs had come on from Southport at noon, and had a fair following of supporters amongst the 6000 present. They had McNaught and Stormont absent from their half-back line, and played Hughes and Jones, while North End had the same side as at London. The 'Spurs captain won the toss, and North End began the play up the incline, and slightly against the wind. They set to work at once, and though the home lot attacked, the 'Spurs forced their way down, and McBride was early called upon. This surprised the home supporters, who were upset at the end of six minutes when the right wing centred and **Cameron** sent in a fast shot which beat McBride, and scored. From the restart North End again took up the attack, but their halves and backs tackled and fed miserably. Time after time they allowed the visitors to have free-kicks, and from a grand run down the right wing **Brown** got a centre and scored the second goal. The North End players lost their heads after this, and before half-time the same player *{Brown}* had put his side still further ahead, and half-way through the 'Spurs led by three goals to love.

On resuming, North End went off with a burst, and Becton scored from a free kick for Morris handling the ball. The game was more even after this, and both custodians saved hot shots. At length Kirwan sent in a capital centre, and **Brown**, getting on the ball, sent in a low shot which beat McBride. The game now appeared all over, but towards the close the home team made a rush, and Pratt scored with a good shot. The 'Spurs were a long way the better team, and fully deserved their win of four goals to two.

RESULT: PRESTON NORTH END 2 - TOTTENHAM HOTSPUR 4

TOTTENHAM: Clawley (goal); Erentz and Tait (backs); Morris, Hughes and Stormont (halves); Smith, Cameron [1], Brown [3], Copeland and Kirwan (forwards).
NORTH END: McBride (goal); Dunn and McMahon (backs); Elliott, McIntyre and Tod (halves); Parker, Gara, Pratt [1], Becton and Green (forwards). [1 anon]
Referee: Mr. A. G. Hines (Nottingham).

SUNDERLAND v. SHEFFIELD UNITED
First Round Proper – Saturday 9th February, 1901
Athletic News - Monday 11th February, 1901
SHEFFIELD UNITED WIN AT SUNDERLAND.
[By Tom Tiddler.]

Sheffield United visited Roker Park, and pulled off the Cup-tie by two to one. This in brief is what happened, and Sunderland's hopes and aspirations are once again nipped in the bud. The contest was brought off in fine, spring-like weather, the day, in fact, being one of the best we have had for about a month, and though the ground was a bit greasy it was not so bad as to spoil the play. Upwards of 26,000 persons paid to see the match, the gate receipts amounting to £849 18s. Sunderland were able to command the services of their best eleven, but Sheffield were in a bit of a quandary owing to Foulke and Johnson being doubtful starters, indeed, it was not until within a few minutes of kicking-off that the eleven was chosen. The United were the first to find their feet, and, in the opening stages, could do nothing wrong. Ten minutes after the start the home defence was slow in clearing, and Lipsham running up with a fast rising shot placed the ball into the net.

LIPSHAM'S FIRST GOAL

This was the first goal Lipsham had scored for the United. Field followed up with a beauty, which Doig had some difficulty in getting away. Sunderland then improved, and seriously menaced the Sheffield defence. A fine cross shot by William Hogg placed the ball right into the goal mouth, and McLatchie rushed up to put it through, but just as he got to the ball Thickett took the feet from under him, and the leather rolled harmlessly by. The referee allowed a penalty. Ferguson shot hard, but Foulke diverted its course. Ferguson quickly pounced upon it and again shot, but the ball struck the post and rebounded into play before a third attempt could be made, and Sheffield saved the situation by granting a corner. However, just before the interval Ferguson placed the ball nicely, and McLatchie dodging round one of the backs put on the equaliser, and at half-time the score was one each.

The second period was for a long while of an even character, the ball travelling regularly up and down the field. Then the home team fairly bustled the Sheffield defenders, gaining three corners in rapid succession. The forwards were weak in front, however, and some good chances were spoiled.

A LATE WINNING GOAL

The flag had just been lowered to indicate that only ten minutes remained for play, when Priest got possession, and racing past the backs put on the winning goal with a fast shot. The ball struck the upright high up, and dropped into the net right out of Doigs reach. Sunderland tried their utmost to retrieve their position, but failed, and had to retire beaten. Whilst heartily congratulating Sheffield on their victory, I must say that they were lucky to win, McLatchie would most certainly have scored had he not been fouled, and this would have counted a draw, to say the least. On the play Sunderland deserved a draw, but no more, for with the exception of the first few minutes Sunderland's general exposition was the better of the two, but this alone is not sufficient to win matches - especially cup-ties. Weak and erratic forward work in front goal was the cause of the defeat, only W. Hogg and Miller playing to their reputation. R. Hogg in particular was very much off. The left wing, too, were not so clever as I have seen them. Ferguson was the cleverest of the halves, but as a line they were not so smart as their opponents. McCrombie was the more reliable of the backs, Watson doing but moderately although he greatly improved in the second half. Doig was not to blame for the shots that beat him. Despite his great weight Foulke showed plenty of activity between the sticks and brought off some really fine saves. Thickett was not so good as his partner, Boyle, who played up in a style that well merited the cap that has just been conferred upon him. He was clean in his work, and has greatly improved since leaving Sunderland. Needham was a hero in himself and easily the best half on the field. His cool and calculating play saved his side repeatedly. The forwards are a sturdy, go ahead, lot, and made no bones about shooting when half a chance presented itself. Bennett was especially dangerous with his fine, dashing runs. He and field made the most effective wing. Hedley seemed slow, but his pacing was good, while Lipsham and Priest worked splendidly together, although the former was too much given to lying offside. The result was a bitter disappointment to the Sunderland crowd, as never before, perhaps, had the supporters been so hopeful of winning as on Saturday.

RESULT: SUNDERLAND 1 – SHEFFIELD UNITED 2

SHEFFIELD: Foulke (goal); Thickett and Boyle (backs); Beers, Morren and Needham (halves); Bennett, Field, Hedley, Priest [1] and Lipsham [1] (forwards).
SUNDERLAND: Doig (goal); McCombie and Watson (backs); Ferguson, McAllister and Farquhar (halves); W. Hogg, R. Hogg, Miller, Livingstone, and McLatchie [1] (forwards).
Referee: Mr. J. Lewis (Blackburn).

PICK OF THE OTHER TIES

Second division Middlesbrough Qualified to reach the First Round proper and an enticing Tyne/Tees tussle with First Division Newcastle United.

MIDDLESBROUGH v. NEWCASTLE UNITED
First Round Proper – Saturday 9th February, 1901
Athletic News - Monday 11th February, 1901
ANOTHER SURPRISE FROM MIDDLESBROUGH

When Middlesbrough entered the Cup competition proper by defeating Grimsby, it is no disparagement to the Tees-siders to say their supporters were surprised, if agreeably so. Of course they do not always rise to the standard reached at Grimsby, and they did not shine in their League games as might have been expected. Yet, as the Newcastle people have said ever since it was known that Newcastle United and Middlesbrough were drawn for the first round, Middlesbrough are not bad cup fighters and now Newcastle United know it to their sorrow. Matters did not seem propitious for Middlesbrough on Saturday morning, for Higgins' (captain) suspension does not expire until today, and it was found that Miller, another half-back and the reserve half-back, McNally, were neither of them fit to play. Then again, at the last moment, Dow, Middlesbrough's best back, and captain *pro tem*, was found equally unfit. Thus Middlesbrough had to enter the field with the two backs who did duty for them in the club's sorrowing days, and Brown, the centre forward, who has been on the sick list for a month, had to go half-back. This gave McCowie a chance of being put into the team, so that Middlesbrough entered the arena with two reserves not previously highly valued. Newcastle, on the other hand, were at full strength. The ground was decidedly soft and heavy, though not so sticky as was expected. When the teams entered the field with 16,000 spectators looking on – there would have been several thousands more if room for them could have been found – it was seen that only Smith, the ex-Notts County man, was taller than the smallest Newcastle man. Here, perhaps, is the secret of Middlesbrough's success. Newcastle are accustomed to playing on a fast ground, and the heavy Middlesbrough turf told more upon them than upon the lighter Tees-siders. During the last five minutes the halves and backs were pretty well worn out and showed signs of distress, while the home team never flagged from beginning to end. The United every now and again forced the pace most vigorously, but Middlesbrough withstood each onslaught, which rarely lasted over four or five minutes, and then they seized their opportunities to wage war vigorously in the visitors' quarters.

THE GAME

Newcastle, losing the toss, had to play against a brilliant sun. McFarlane, the swift outside right of the visitors, soon got possession, and he looked like opening the scoring, but the ball was intercepted and Middlesbrough raced away, Moran finally shooting just wide of the post. A foul gave Newcastle another chance, and Frail had to fist out. So far honours were even, but the home team grew more troublesome, and Kingsley had to make use of all his skill to return the smart shots sent straight for goal. During the whole of the first half Middlesbrough sent in more shots at goal than Newcastle, and they were on the whole more dangerous than the abortive attempts of the Newcastle men. The Tynesiders were certainly fleeter of foot and had rare command of the ball, but somehow they never seemed during the first half to get into their favourite position for shooting. Peddie once or twice put in a good shot, but it lacked it's usual sting, Frail was lucky perhaps to save from A. Gardner, as he thrust out his fist in time to divert a shot that even then might have sailed into the net. It looked all through the first half as if the interval would arrive goalless, but two minutes from time a corner fell to Middlesbrough, and Wardrope centring well therefrom, **Robertson** just headed over Kingsley's head. The cheering and enthusiasm beggared description.

THE SECOND HALF

Restarting, Newcastle went away with a terrific rush. The passing of the forward line was a revelation to Middlesbrough spectators, and Peddie got in one of his final shots, only, however, to have it promptly cleared. Middlesbrough allowed Newcastle to have their spurt, and then responded in no less spirited fashion, if not as prettily. At any rate they scored, Moran receiving from Smith, who had played a half-back game unequal to any on the field, eluded Carr and Gardner, swinging the ball across the goal, and finding Wardrope in position to shoot smartly into the net. Middlesbrough spectators rubbed their eyes as they cheered, for, truth to tell, they did not expect this of their pets. Straight from the kick-off Newcastle tried another of their grand rushes, and this time it luckily came off, for Aiken caught a good attempt to clear, and returned smartly between the posts. This, of course, made the game more interesting, for Newcastle pressed with might and main, keeping to the home quarters for fully five minutes, without shooting as frequently as they might, but looking extremely dangerous. Turn and turn about, however, Middlesbrough again proved how how keenly aggressive they could be. McCowie, who had more than justified his inclusion, sent in one of his stinging shots, striking Gardner, the Newcastle back, and shooting into goal. Three goals to one! The victory of the home team seemed sure now, particularly as the efforts of Newcastle got weaker. The visitors tried to force the Tees-siders to defend, and the backs seized a chance to get half-way up the field, but they soon regretted the step. Middlesbrough wisely considered that aggressiveness was the better defence, and they laiud themselves out to keep the Newcastle halves and backs busy, thereby forcing the visitors of both divisions to work for any advance made. The Newcastle football scribes had proved better prophets than Middlesbrough had dared to hope. Possibly none were more surprised at the result than the Middlesbrough directors, whose string of disappointments had probably caused them to abandon all hope of success. But yet Middlesbrough have shown once more that they can rise to the occasion, if they cannot prove themselves equal to uniform success.

RESULT: MIDDLESBROUGH 3 – NEWCASTLE UNITED 1

MIDDLESBROUGH: Frail (goal); Dow and Ramsay (backs); Miller, Smith and McNally (halves); Moran, McCowie [1], Robertson [1], Brown and Wardrope [1] (forwards).
NEWCASTLE UTD: Kingsley (goal); Burgess and D. Gardner (backs); Ghee, Aitken [1] and Carr (halves); McFarlane, A. Gardner, Peddie, Laidlaw and Fraser. (forwards).
Referee: anon ().

F.A. CUP - SECOND ROUND

The second round ties were scheduled to be played on 23rd February, 1901. The sixteen remaining sides were made up of: 9 from Division One (Aston Villa, Bolton Wand., Bury, Everton, Notts. County, Notts Forest, Sheffield Utd., West Bromwich Alb. and Wolverhampton Wand); 4 from Division Two (Burnley, Middlesbrough, Small Heath, Woolwich Arsenal) and 3 from the Southern League (Kettering, Reading and Tottenham).

'Spurs were the only one of the three Southern League teams to be drawn at home but had, perhaps, the toughest encounter against the holders, Bury, currently in their best form and chasing hard for the First Division Championship title (third in the table, two points behind the leaders but with a game in hand.) Reading were away to First Division strugglers Bolton Wanderers - who, up to date, had scored fewer goals than any other club in that division – whilst Kettering looked to have the best chance of progressing at mid-table Second Division Middlesbrough.

Anticipation in North London for 'Spurs encounter with the holders was at fever pitch, and with a huge crowd expected, the club brought in a gang of labourers who spent much of the preceding week raising the cinder path that encircled the pitch in order to accommodate more spectators, whilst the Great Eastern Railway put on extra trains to bring them in from the suburbs.. The team, meanwhile, who had been training at home since the previous Sunday, spent the last night before the match together at the Forest Hotel in Chingford, from where they were to be taken direct to the ground at the last possible hour.

Bury played 10 of the side that won them the cup the previous year and were the clear favourites to go forward. The 'London Evening Standard' (22/02/1901) commented:

"… we come to what may be, after all, if Tottenham Hotspur rise to the occasion, the tit-bit of this second round; for Bury visit them, and victory over the clever Cup-holders would undoubtedly be the greatest event of the day. The "Spurs" will try hard; but the dash and sound defence of the Bury eleven are well known, and we expect they will win by a small margin."

TOTTENHAM HOTSPUR v. BURY
Second Round Proper – Saturday 23rd February, 1901
Athletic News - Monday 25th February, 1901
A HOT 'UN AT TOTTENHAM - CUP-HOLDERS BEATEN ON THEIR MERITS.
[By The Old Athlete.]

Apart from Cup finals, I cannot recall a match which excited more interest in the London district than the meeting of Hotspur and Bury. For the last few days, go where you would, you would always hear the probabilities of the game being discussed. On Saturday all roads seemed to lead Tottenham, and despite the excellent service put on by the Great Eastern Company, so great was the demand for seats that all the trains, which were despatched at intervals of few minutes, were packed to their utmost capacity. It was quite an hour before the time advertised for the start when I reached the ground, and then it seemed full, but people continued to pour in until, when the ball was started, there must hare been considerably over 20,000 people present. The surroundings were everything that could be desired, save that the ground was perhaps a little too soft, but this is only to be expected at this season of the year. Bury were, of course, strong favourites, although the supporters of the Hotspurs' professed to be very hopeful. I fancy, even making every allowance for their meritorious victory over Preston, it was case of the wish, in many cases, being father to the thought. With regard to the teams, the Cup-holders brought up their full strength, but Hotspur did not make their final selection till the eleventh hour, when it was decided to leave out McNaught and Stormont in favour of Hughes and Jones.

A SENSATIONAL START.

The match commenced rather tamely, but the 'Spurs were the first to attack, and McEwan, who all through gave a superb display of defensive play, stopped Smith and Cameron, who were getting dangerously close. He passed the ball right across to Richards, who dashed away down the right, and, putting in front of goal, Sagar. after a bit of a mull, sent the ball into the net before a couple of minutes had expired. Almost immediately afterwards Richards had another chance, but kicked across the mouth of the goal when he had no one to stop him but Clawley. This made the followers of Hotspur look very glum, but it did not affect the players much, as they worked tremendously hard, and after good piece of combined play a trimmer by Copeland gave Thompson some trouble. The home side had now settled down, and were playing a really good, hard game, the half-backs especially doing well, and kept repeatedly stopping the rushes of the Bury forwards, of whom Sagar and Richards were very prominent. Now and again they would break clear, but they seldom got dangerous, while once Brown broke through, and lost a good chance by a rather feeble shot.

HOTSPUR IMPROVE.

Hotspur were now showing decidedly the better form, and it required the best that the Bury backs could do to keep them away. The pace was now tremendously fast, but the shooting was very wild on the part of the 'Spurs, who sent the ball almost everywhere but into the net. Once a long shot by Hughes very nearly equalised. About a quarter of an hour before the change Hotspur seemed to slacken a little - no wonder at the pace they had been travelling - and the visitors became more prominent, Sagar and Richards especially so. Erentz, who was very sure throughout, distinguished himself by clearing away a brilliant centre the latter, which fell about a yard front of the goal, when McLuckie was only about two or three yards away. Rose, who played a rather rough fame, was penalised for fouling, and from the kick away went the 'Spur's forwards to the other end. Again McEwan, who was undoubtedly the best back on the field, cleared in grand style. lot of give-and-take play followed, but once when he had the Bury goal open **Brown** skied the ball, though he atoned for his mistake a minute later when he got a beautiful pass from Cameron past Thompson, who had no chance of stopping it. And didn't the 'Spurs" go after this, while the cheering all round was tremendous. With a less capable goalkeeper than Thompson opposed to them, the home side might have easily scored again, but they crossed over with honours equal.

Bury, who were without Ross, who had been slightly injured, were acting mainly on the defensive after resuming for some time, but on his return they again attacked. The combination of the forwards, however, was bad. Clawley came in for a round of applause for saving shots from Plant and Richards, both stingers.

THE WINNING GOAL

The pressure on the 'Spurs lines was not of long duration, as a very pretty combined run by Kirwan and Copeland, who worked exceedingly well together, took the ball to the other end. Richards next got almost clear, outpacing all his rivals except Erentz and got dangerously close ere the latter was obliged to kick behind, while Sagar immediately afterwards slipped up when he looked like scoring. The attack died out soon after, and Hotspur once more assumed the offensive. Kirwan started it with a fine run, which was repeated by Smith, on the other wing, directly after, and the latter dropping the ball in front of goal, **Brown** rushed up and heading through gave his side what proved to be the winning point. This again set the Spurs going at express pace, and Brown might easily have scored another goal had he not, in the excitement of the moment, fisted the ball in. Bury towards the close were playing anything but a clean game, and twice narrowly escaped having a penalty given against them. They made one last desperate attempt in the last five minutes, but the defence of the 'Spurs was equal to the occasion, and they retired amidst the applause of the assembled thousands with a well-deserved victory by 2 goals to 1.

OBSERVATIONS

For a Cup-tie, it was one of the best games that has ever been played at Tottenham. It was vigorous without being unduly rough, and the home side, who had considerably the better of it. owe their success almost entirely to their superior combination, and the smart work done by their half-backs, who were far and away better than the Bury second line. The visitors' forwards, though individually Sagar and Richards did some good things, never seemed to get fairly together, especially being considerably below his usual form. Darroch was not altogether safe, but too much praise cannot be accorded to McEwan, whose defence all through the piece was as good as anybody could wish to see, and seriously interfered with the combination of both Smith and Cameron, who did not appear to work too well together. The other 'Spurs wing, Kirwan and Copeland, were very good, but I have seen Brown play better, although he scored both the goals. Hughes was certainly the best half on the field, and Jones also did a lot of really good work. To this pair a lot of the credit of breaking up the Bury combination belongs. Tait was not too sure, but this remark does not apply to Erentz, who was very safe, and played as coolly as if nothing depended on the result of the match. Both goalkeepers were at their best. The victory of the 'Spurs it is needless to say, has given immense satisfaction all through the south, and is they can only maintain the form they showed on Saturday, when they played a thorough Cup game, the return of the Cup to the south appears within measurable distance.

RESULT: TOTTENHAM HOTSPUR 2 - BURY 1

TOTTENHAM: Clawley (goal); Erentz and Tait (backs); Morris, Hughes and Jones (halves); Smith, Cameron, Brown [2], Copeland and Kirwan (forwards).
BURY: Thompson (goal); Darroch and McEwan (backs); Pray, Leeming and Ross (halves); Richards, Wood, McLuckie, Sagar [1] and Plant (forwards).
Referee: Mr. A. Green (West Bromwich).

Midway through the match a great cheer went up - and was carried on in scenes of jubilation which continued around the whole ground for several minutes – all of which was nothing to do with the play upon the field. Instead, news had filtered into the ground of the newspaper banners being paraded outside. Leading Boer general Christiaan Rudolf de Wet's invasion of Cape Colony had been shattered at Middelburg by a British relief column and his army put to flight!

On the football field, Tottenham's was the result of the round:

The 'London Evening Standard' (25/02/1901):
Of all Saturday's performances, the best was undoubtedly that of Tottenham Hotspur, who gained the coveted distinction of being the team to knock out (2-1) the Cup-holders, the crack Bury side. There was no question as to the "Spurs" fully deserving their victory; for, making due allowance for the injury to Ross, the Bury half-back, they were certainly the smarter team on the day's play. Indeed, so capital a show did they make that we do not hesitate to say that, if they can maintain this form they should have as good a chance as any club in the country of winning the Cup this year.

SHEFFIELD UNITED v. EVERTON
Second Round Proper – Saturday 23rd February, 1901
Athletic News - Monday 25th February, 1901
GREAT DAY FOR SHEFFIELD
[By Nondescript]

UNITED STILL STAND

Another Liverpool ship went down on Saturday, entailing a loss of all hands and a cargo of best hopes which had been grown for some years on the Goodison plantations. 'Tis marvellous what they can not do at the seaport. One bargained for the red-shirted pirates of Anfield-road being sent to an early grave, but the idea was very largely subscribed to that the steadier going blues would have a much pleasanter passage. It was not to be, however, and another wreck on the Bramall sands has to be added to the list. In this case it was the more disastrous because it was not altogether expected, and quite a large party came through from the West Coast in hopes of at least seeing the craft float off without damage. It really seems, however, as if those Liverpool sports who follow football will be grey whiskered and bent with age before the Cup - which jeers and not exuberates - comes home. Worse teams than those which fluttered the colours last weekend have, it is true, won matches at a much earlier stage in the competition, but in being thus removed on Saturday they have no other reason to advance than that they were not equal to the task in hand. No, the luck has been out this time round, and they and their neighbours on the other side of Stanley Park will have to begin all over again. Having said so much on the one hand, let me extend the other to Sheffield United, and congratulate them heartily on once again reaching the last eight. Now that the only team which could have beaten them, to wit, Bury, have gone under, they may reckon themselves as good as any of the opposition remaining, and for neither virtuous Villan or Forrester bold, nor eke the brightest star in the Southern firmament need they entertain anything more than due respect. I daren't say anything further in their favour, lest it should lead to their undoing. I have already picked in turn Blackburn rovers and Bury to win this cup, and both have played me false. Nowadays you only need to get the idea into your head that a certain team will do this, that, and the other thing, and they throw you over at the first time of asking. Stranger things have happened than that the "Wolves" and Middlesbrough should be travelling up to the Christians' Palace this April.

ABOUT THE GAME

If I might be allowed to put in another chip of nautical metaphor, the United won on Saturday because they proved the better navigators. "Navvies" would fit the situation just as aptly. The top off the ground, which was so loose that it threatened to come off in places, afforded every opportunity for a fellow with figure skating proclivities, and contortionist footballers were tickling the humour of the crowd every other minute. After describing all sorts of geometric designs on the soft carpet, down a player would come "splosh" on all fours without any assistance, and although the field was strictly impartial in it's dirty behaviour to the combatants, I suppose the excuse advanced by the beaten side would be that anything could happen under such circumstances. This, however, while a consoling reflection to some folks, will not diminish the force of the argument that Sheffield, as things went, played better football - stronger football, at any rate. Prior to the kick off the visitors indulged in a few minutes target practice which must have had a very intimidating influence on the local populace, for the former were scoring bulls eyes with nearly every shot. But this is precisely what they did not do when the serious conflict began, and on such occasions as the United backs allowed them to get on speaking terms with Foulke, the giant was by no means sorely beset. He ought to have been placed in difficulties - should have been beaten in fact - but that is another matter.

HOW THE UNITED WON

Before anything was scored Taylor sent a ball begging across the goalmouth, and then Sharp failed to judge a not over difficult ball at a favourable range and was remiss again. Mistakes not only prevented Everton from scoring themselves, but also contributed largely to the two goals by which they were beaten. It was thus wise: after half an hour United had a free kick for offside, not far from midfield. Boyle, who had all along distinguished himself, placed the ball well to the right of the posts, and with Abbott and Eccles both failing to circumvent Bennett, that worthy found the best part of an open goal to go at, and accordingly captured it. Previously Eccles had evoked a hearty burst of cheering by chasing and pulling up Bennett and Field with one of the best bits of tackling ever seen on a ground. In the case of the second Proudfoot and Settle were both dallying with the ball, with the result that Thickett crashed between the pair. Bennett got possession, and worked beautifully past Eccles, dribbled on, and, though hampered again, got in his last stride and a beauty of a shot attached to it, with the result that, as before, Muir had not a chance. That effectually settled the issue, as although there were twenty five minutes still to go Everton were a beaten team. Previously they had shown good fight, albeit a lot more faulty footwork than the state of the ground was responsible for. They had, at any rate, kept their followers in a state of expectancy, and, be it said, they came desperately near scoring, while their full backs were also permitted to hammer away at Foulke from long range. It was from a well placed kick by Eccles that an opportunity stared at least two of the inside forwards in the face, but the only result was a gigantic scrimmage on the line, in which Foulke played the part of Horatio[10]. A claim was indeed made that the ball had been through. Even if it had it would not have counted, for the referee had detected some breach of rules which was not quite clear at such a distance from the stand. Another time Sharp - one of the very few occasions when he outwitted Boyle - had a clear run, but to the dismay of his colleagues he slipped, and went land-measuring when in full cry for goal.

---

10 A reference to Horatio Cocles – an ancient Roman hero who single-handedly held back an army of invaders from crossing a narrow bridge whilst his comrades tore it down behind him.

This was indeed hard luck, and both these events it should be said occurred ere the United had made themselves tolerably sure of victory. Afterwards Everton, save for a few individual bursts, fell off, and United while not exerting themselves to the far end, were just as near scoring again. Further, they were carrying a passenger for the greater part of the concluding half. Field happening to meet with a collision which did him no good at all.

THE PLAYERS

For an hour there was not such a great disparity between the teams, although it must be said the United went about their work in a straighter fashion, and lasted sufficiently well to give a fine advertisement to the invigorating qualities of the air of Skegness. On such a day it was quite possible for a player to do his level best and find his efforts come all awry, and one's criticism need not accordingly be too pointed, although it has to be said that there were some conspicuous successes, just as there were some noticeable failures. One of the most prominent men on the winning side was Boyle, who also played a scrupulously fair game. Another was Bennett, who carried the Everton goal on the second occasion by sheer force of individual effort. It was one of the "Mexborough particulars," and at times he is very great on them. When he rises to Saturday's form, and throws aside the mantle of the moody Dane, he is the most dangerous right-winger in the country. Thickett was in fine feather, and indeed the backs on both sides acquitted themselves with credit, Balmer kicking as stoutly as any, and Eccles frequently doing very clever work, though both goals came from his side. In the two intermediate lines Needham stood out, as he usually does when judgement above everything else is an essential. Johnson, playing better than we have previously seen him this season, was every whit as good as Wolstenhulme, though for the sake of consistency, not to mention immunity from injuries, the last named of the pair could not well be left out of the International trial match. Booth's one fault was that he was prone to finesse at times, and he lost good ground by doing so. Abbott was solid throughout; Morren occasionally wild, but as persevering as ever. Hedley pleased me very much, and he gets a chance today at London to show his paces before a critical crowd. So, too, does Proudfoot earn a mark of favour on the other side. but Sharp was disappointing, and the whole Everton line did not piece up as well as their opponents, who read the more dangerous when swinging along, and troubled the goalkeeper far oftener. On a dry patch the visitors would probably have given a different account of themselves. They didn't perform badly, but they lost to a better team. I should add that the contest was fought with good feeling, and smart official rulings on the offside business were another gratifying feature. When the free kick was signalled from which the United scored their first goal, it was a very fine point, but the decision was undoubtedly correct.

RESULT: SHEFFIELD UNITED 2 – EVERTON 0

SHEFFIELD UTD: Foulke (goal); Thickett and Boyle (backs); Johnson, Morren and Needham (halves); Bennet [2], Field, Hedley, Priest and Lipsham (forwards).
EVERTON: Muir (goal); Balmer and Eccles (backs); Wolstenholme, Booth and Abbott (halves); Sharp, Taylor, Proudfoot, Settle and Turner (forwards).
Referee: Mr. A. G. Kingscott

PICK OF THE OTHER TIES

The standout draw of the second round was the West Midlands v. East Midlands tie between Aston Villa and Nottingham Forest, which, indeed turned out to be full of incident.

ASTON VILLA v. NOTTINGHAM FOREST
Second Round Proper – Saturday 23rd February, 1901
Athletic News - Monday 25th February, 1901
A GREAT GAME AT BIRMINGHAM
[By The Free Critic.]

The match of the round was universally accepted as Aston Villa v. Nottingham Forest, for here we had last year's League champions meeting the favourites for the current season's honours of the League. Not only so, but the Forest have shown such consistently good form away from home - their great weakness of a year or two back - that the advantage of ground did not give the Villa so much of a pull. Immediately the result of the draw became known, preparations for the reception of a big crowd were commenced. But the compact and complete arrangements at Aston necessitate comparatively little trouble in this direction. Still it was necessary to do something in view of the huge gathering expected, and this something was done. The secretary, George Ramsey, very early on wore a worried look, although it was caused by what many secretaries would consider the congenial task of issuing high-priced tickets. The Midland Railway Company had arranged for cheap fares from several stations in Lancashire, probably chiefly owing to the fact that the Burnley team were due in Birmingham to meet Small Heath. On board was Mr. John Lewis who was down referee the big match, and, indeed, the train out of Victoria Station[11] was completely packed. The weather was none too promising, but brightened up considerably as we passed through Derbyshire. At Derby we came across the Foresters looking as fit and well as their saloon - a handsome vehicle - and we were comfortable until reaching Tamworth, where as soon as the train pulled up - indeed, a little before - we were "invested," but by most agreeable companions, if patriotic Tamworthians, and heard the praises of the town in full, and also all the local gossip, and from what one intelligent, determined-looking gentleman said, someone will have a hot time at Tamworth tomorrow evening for daring to assert that the factory girls the town would not make as good wives as the general servants. It is wonderful what peculiar discussions arise in a railway carriage. However, we landed at New-street in fair time, and everyone appeared to talking about the football match.

TO THE GROUND

It was a bit uncertain whether we could procure a vehicle, but the military looking gentleman in charge of the Colonade Hotel promptly satisfied us on this point, and in a few moments announced that the carriage awaited us or words to that effect. There was either something wrong with the construction of the conveyance - Mr. Lewis, as an expert, said there was - or the streets were too muddy, or perhaps it was a

---

11   Manchester Victoria.

combination, but be that as it may we had to dodge the fleeting mud drops all the way down.

ON THE GROUND

That, however, is a detail, and once inside the enclosure everything was as comfortably arranged as 'twas possible. The members of the International Selection Committee had intimated their desire to be present, and the best seats on the ground were offered them, whilst immediately opposite were the members of the Forest Committee. It was very pleasant, despite a considerable number of noisy ejaculations the part of our old friend, Charlie Johnson, who was determined to captain the Villa from the stand. But, he sagely remarked: "They can't hear me, and it relieves my feelings." From the stentorian voice I doubt the first part of the statement, but then I was immediately below him, and got the full force of the instructions. The cheaper part of the ground, that is the embankment behind the goals, was apparently packed half an hour before the start, but still people rolled up in hundreds, and they seemed quite comfortable. The price for the stand opposite the principal one bad been doubled, but that was fairly well filled, and the only slack spot was in the cycling track. Everything was of the most orderly character, and one thing to admire in the Villa directorate is their thoroughness. One may not always agree with their methods, but they generally have very good reasons for what they do. At the time of writing I do not know the numbers, but I should say there were between 40,000 and 50,000 present. We had a silver band marching around, and if it partakes somewhat of the show business, it does not the slightest harm, and certainly serves to pass away the time. The teams looked very fit and well, and both had a hearty cheer as they stepped on the ground at full strength, the Forest apparently holding the advantage so far as physique went, and they are indeed a fine lot of young fellows.

AN UNFORTUNATE ACCIDENT

It was early evident that we were in for a hard determined, game, and although the play was fairly even during the first quarter of an hour, the Foresters struck me as being the more aggressive lot, for they were continually on the ball, and the Villa made the mistake of keeping it in the air, for anyone who is acquainted with their style of play knows perfectly well that they want it on the ground. Besides, the Forest possess some tall fellows who have useful heads on their shoulders. The Forest had the first piece of bad luck, for Calvey rushed in and missed heading a beautiful centre from the right. This would not have mattered very much, for Morris, I think it was, pounced on the ball and shot straight for goal, wide of George, but unfortunately in his headlong rush, Calvey had not managed to get over the line, and, worse than all, stopped the ball just as it was going through. It was, of course, offside. Immediately after this a most unfortunate accident happened. Linacre had a shot to save, cleared, Johnson got the ball and had a glorious chance of shooting, but passed. From a Forest point of view this particular part of the proceedings was perfectly agreeable, but Frank Forman, scenting danger, went for Johnson, and Norris coming across him, had his leg broken just above the ankle. It was soon evident that something of a serious nature had happened, for the players clustered round, doctors were summoned. and the worst appeared probable when the ambulance was taken on the ground. Norris being conveyed to the referee's room, and alter an official pronouncement Mr. Ancell, the Villa president, went to a lot trouble in order to procure a horse ambulance to convey Norris to the General Hospital. Indeed the whole of the Villa officials were most kind and considerate, and although Norris asked if it were not possible to get him to Preston he may rest assured he will be well looked after in Birmingham. He is a typical Lancashire lad, and took matters quite philosophically, comforted by the veteran McPherson. Whilst I was away with Norris I was told that the Villa had a desperate scrimmage in the Forest goal, and that Linacre saved when the ball was over the line, but Mr. Lewis afterwards said had no doubt about it being a legitimate clearance. The Villa had unquestionably the best of matters, as could only be expected, for Forman put Capes at half-back and played four forwards. I was pleased he didn't play the one back game. Those four forwards often proved troublesome, and could not be treated with the slightest amount of disrespect. But the bulk of the play was at the other end. and the pressure only served to bring out the plucky defensive powers of the Forest.

POOR SHOOTING

The Villa could not be accused of deadly shooting, and although the ball was once netted Smith was clean off-side. Morris got away on the left wing, and looked extremely dangerous. but it came to nought, and the best shot on the Villa side was one by Wilkes who gathered the ball beautifully, ran along, and just at the right moment, sent in a low one which Linacre had to dart forward to at full length. However, he saved, and we proceeded merrily along with the Villa pressing, but the Forest forwards always to reckoned with, until half-time, when neither goalkeeper had been beaten.

INTERESTING SECOND HALF

Frank Forman was greatly upset at the accident he had unwittingly been the cause of, and seemed to feel it very much, as was only natural under the circumstances. In this respect he seemed more cut up than did Norris, who would have liked to remain until the finish, but had to go. The Forest now had what slight wind there was, and played one of the most plucky games I have seen. They wisely bestowed great care on their lines of defence, and the Villa did not seem to adapt themselves to the position of affairs, for they did too much passing and too little rushing, with the result that the dashing Foresters were always ready for the ball and cleared. Then Calvey and his worthy trio lay pretty well up, and once on the ball they went away in a manner which invariably meant trouble, and speaking generally I should say they were quite as dangerous their opponents. Morris in particular, all alone the left wing as he was, put in exceedingly clever work, and the impartial crowd cheered again and again as the Reds bore down on the Villa goal. It was a big struggle, but the Forest lasted the better of the two teams, and during the last quarter of an hour were more likely to score than were their opponents, although the Villa had one or two good opportunities, and in the last five minutes, from a corner, Linacre effected a splendid save, but the end came without any scoring, the gallant ten having a hearty reception as they reached the stand. And they deserved it.

A BRIEF CRITICISM

The most enthusiastic Villa supporter could not withhold a word of admiration for the Foresters, who at the start knew the magnitude of their task, and afterwards had it increased ten-fold by the enforced absence of Norris. But it was just here that their pluck and determination came in. They faced the unequal task like men, and came out trumps. That is to say they averted defeat, and now have the chance of meeting the Villa at Nottingham. They are a fine team in every way. Well-built young fellows, with a fair turn of speed, intelligent knowledge of the game, and invariably on the job, they are worthy of being League champions as well as Cup-holders. Without depreciating the other members of his side, Frank Forman was the outstanding figure, and England has no need to look further for a centre half-back. But the others were all good, and Calvey is a centre of a rather laborious, but eminently useful, type, and knows what to do with the ball when gets it. Their cleverest forward is Morris, the Welsh International, and he is an artist. The backs don't stop at anything - they realise it is their duty to clear and they clear, whilst the goalkeeper is a worthy successor to Allsopp. The Villa were disappointing especially in two important details - their lasting powers and their shooting abilities. The forwards passed and passed when they ought to have shot and shot. Smith was the best of the lot and gave several of his old time dribbles, but on the whole the forward line must be described an ineffective one. Cowan was the most prominent of the halves, although Wilkes struck one as being most promising, but even the middle line was not up to the Villa standard. At back Evans easily took first place, and is one of the very best we have. George had not many opportunities of displaying his cleverness, but when he had did not give his side away. It was a most enjoyable match, kept well in hand by Mr. Lewis, who refereed as well as ever, and the two linesmen, although they possess rather unpronounceable names, carried out their duties efficiently.

RESULT: ASTON VILLA 0 – NOTTINGHAM FOREST 0

ASTON VILLA: George (goal); Spencer and Evans (backs); Bowman, Cowan and Wilkes (halves); Athersmith, Devey, Johnson, Garratty and Smith (forwards).
NOTTINGHAM FOREST: Linacre (goal); Peers and Iremonger (backs); G. Robinson, F. Forman and Norris (halves); F.R. Forman, Murray, Calvey, Morris and Capes (forwards).
Referee: Mr. J. Lewis (Blackburn)

NOTTINGHAM FOREST v. ASTON VILLA
Replay – Wednesday 27th February, 1901
The Sportsman - Thursday 28th February, 1901
THE VILLA WIN AN EXCITING MATCH

At Nottingham, yesterday, something like 27,000 spectators witnessed the decision of this replayed Cup-tie. The Villa team was the same as at Birmingham, and Forrest completed their side (in the absence of Norris, who sustained a broken leg in the first match) with Spouncer, Capes playing half-back. The latter, it may be said, justified the confidence reposed in him. The ground was in capital condition, and a fast game was witnessed, though it was the Villa team which set the pace, contrary to the expectations of the home spectators, who relied on the reports of the Saturday's game. The first half was brilliant, though slightly in favour of the Villa. Yet the visitors to Nottingham crossed over a goal to the bad, Forest having scored by Spouncer after just half an hour's play. The ball was put off the right wing following a free kick, and Crabtree, busy in looking after Morris, let Spouncer into the net from three yards distance, George very evidently being taken by surprise. The play on both sides was very alert after this, the Foresters showing an inclination to roughness.

In the second half the Villa showed better combination and staying powers than the Foresters, but the home backs were good. However, Iremonger, with his usual recklessness, tripped Devey badly, though he had measured the distance just outside the penalty line, Cowan scored from Crabtree's pass on the free kick being taken, and the teams were level, one goal each, at the end of ninety minutes, the Villa having shown better play, but weak and hesitating shooting.

The extra half hour proved the Foresters to be a shattered team, and Garratty scoring in four minutes, the Foresters were only occasionally dangerous afterwards. They tried all sorts of maneuvers, but to no effect. Just before the close Devey dribbled down and got a third goal, and the result of a fiercely contested match was Aston Villa three goals, Notts. Forest one. It was singular that Linacre had only once to save in the first half, and George had little to do the whole of the game. His most arduous work was in the extra half hour, when he cleared twice superbly.

RESULT: NOTTINGHAM FOREST 1 - ASTON VILLA 3

ASTON VILLA: George (goal); Spencer and Evans (backs); Bowman, Cowan [1] and Wilkes (halves); Athersmith, Devey [1], Johnson, Garratty [1] and Smith (forwards).
NOTTINGHAM FOREST: Linacre (goal); Peers and Iremonger (backs); G. Robinson, F. Forman and Capes (halves); F.R. Forman, Murray, Calvey, Morris and Spouncer [1] (forwards).
Referee: Mr. J. Lewis (Blackburn)

The Aston Villa v. Nottingham Forest tie produced two of the three highest gates of the round. The largest attendance was the 50,000 at the original match, whilst the 27,000 who saw the replay constituted the third highest number. Total gate receipts for the first match amounted to £1,789 (avg 8½d).

'Spurs drew an attendance of 21,000 but by raising their prices for the event were not far behind in gate receipts at £1,330 (Avg. 1s.3d [15d]).

F.A. CUP - THIRD ROUND (Quarter Finals)

The last two remaining Southern League clubs were drawn together with the 'Spurs paying a visit to the 'Biscuitmen' (Reading) at Elm Park. The former offered their hosts the grand sum of £500 for the transfer of home rights but the Berkshire club declined the offer, preferring to go ahead and play the game on their own Elm Park ground. To that end they copied 'Spurs example of the previous round in raising their prices and raising a large cinder bank behind the Tilehurst goal to accommodate extra spectators. For the 'Spurs fans, cheap excursion trains were run from Paddington.

READING v. TOTTENHAM HOTSPUR
Third Round Proper – Saturday 25th March, 1901
Athletic News - Monday 25th February, 1901
HONOURS EVEN AT READING.
[By Biscuit Boy.]

There are no two teams in the South of England who show such a remarkable even record as Reading and Tottenham Hotspur. Prior to Saturday's engagement in the English Cup-tie the clubs had met six times this season, in two friendlies, the same number of Western league engagements and a couple of Southern League matches. Reading won one friendly and drew the other. The Western League fixtures favoured Tottenham in-as-much as one game fell to them and they drew in the other, while in the Southern League contests honours were divided, each having won one match. Moreover, as each club had registered ten goals it was pretty generally recognised that there would a tough battle at Elm Park on Saturday. This combined with the fact that the weather was fine and that each club was expected to place full strength in the field, had a fine effect on the football loving public of the South, who turned up in their thousands. To be accurate 14,417 were accounted for at the turnstiles, and in plump figures the clubs will divide £919 up to now - not bad this for the South. At the last moment it was announced that Mr. Adams, the originally appointed referee, could not act, this gentleman being down with a wrenched knee, but Mr. Green ably "deputised." The enthusiasm was intense - extraordinary if you like - and as the game progressed the urging of the respective partisans became deafening, but fortunately the rival forces showed the best of temper. There was nothing between them beyond a bit of pleasant banter, with nobody upset.

HOW THE PLAY WENT

There was but little wind blowing, and that was directing itself across the ground, and was no advantage to anybody. No sooner had we started than it was seen that we were in for cup-tie football. Tottenham, who are undoubtedly clever, were given a chance in the very first minute of the game to become prominent, but a nice pass to Smith was lost through the flying right-winger being over anxious. This gave Clinch his opportunity, and he didn't fail to seize it. On he came, and the ball was sailing away in the direction of the Spurs' stronghold. Erentz and Tait, however, were equal to the demand, and the former came in for a great cheer for getting in a ponderous kick.

Loose play followed, and neither side could get going in the form know them be equal to. Consequently the scoring sheet had still to be troubled. At length - it seemed a long time, but, as a matter of fact, little more than ten minutes had elapsed - Reading took a free kick, and after finessing before the goal the ball came out to Evans, who, switching himself on to it, sent in a beauty, and there was something approaching an earthquake when it was seen that Clawley was beaten. Far from having a deterrent effect on the play of the Spurs, this encouraged them the more to buckle to with greater gusto. Their forwards showed improved play, and Kirwan, Copeland and Brown, who hitherto appeared unable to set themselves going, now ably assisted Cameron and Smith, and the Reading goal was hotly bombarded. Twice Smith had the appearance of getting on the spot, but although he failed once he forced corner, which Bull rather cleverly cleared. Clinch, too, was doing well amongst the Reading defenders, and Henderson, Mainman and Watts were not a long way behind him. Towards the interval the locals went great guns. Evans and Barnes in turn being particularly dangerous, but with no further score accruing, Reading crossed over leading by a goal to nothing.

A CLEVER EQUALISER

One need not dilate at length on the latter moiety. Play ruled fast certainly, but it was not very edifying, fouls being preqnant. After Cotton had brought off a rather weak clearance, up came the Spurs again, and **Kirwan** screwed in a shot which very properly equalised. It was a really great effort, and well deserved to register the equaliser. Cotton certainly handled the ball, but might just at as well have had a cannon shot to deal with for all that he could with it, as after leaving his hands it nearly forced its way through the webbing at the rear of the net. There was more scoring, and this being so one each was the result, though towards the close Reading ought to have been conceded a penalty kick, for it struck me that Tait deliberately fisted the ball away when Clawley had left his charge. The referee, however, failed to see the transgression, and thus the matter ended. I don't want to mince matters, and should say that neither club deserved to win, for they played well, though each exhibited robustness. Cameron, Smith and Kirwan were decidedly the pick of the Tottenham forwards, and Morris', Hughes, Erentz and Clawley were the pick of the rear guard. Tait has seldom played a weaker game, and Jones apparently did not know what make of Evans, Reading's dashing outside right, who was well supported by Logan. Barnes was good at times, while Mainman was prominent of the halves, Bull and Watts being below par, but Henderson and Clinch, particularly the latter, did finely at back, whilst Cotton was clever in goal.

RESULT: READING 1 - TOTTENHAM HOTSPUR 1

TOTTENHAM: Clawley (goal); Erentz and Tait (backs); Morris, Hughes and Jones (halves); Smith, Cameron, Brown, Copeland and Kirwan [1] (forwards).
READING: Cotton (goal); Henderson and Clinch (backs); Bull, Mainman and Watts (halves); Evans [1], Logan, Pegg, Barnes and A. Sharp (forwards).
Referee: Mr. A. Green (West Bromwich).

READING F.C.

19/03/1901

Cotton
Henderson Mainman Clinch
Bull Logan Pegg Sharp Watts
Evans Barnes

TOTTENHAM HOTSPUR v. READING
Third Round Proper REPLAY – Thursday 28th March, 1901
Morning Post - Friday 25th February, 1901

At Tottenham yesterday the second meeting of the Hotspur with Reading in the third round of the Association cup resulted in a decisive victory for the home team by three goals to none. All round the winners were the stronger, but for their success they had their forwards chiefly to thank. Brown, in the centre, played quite brilliantly, passing cleverly to his wings and showing great dash near goal. He received excellent support from Kirwan and Copeland, on the left, and Cameron and Smith, on the right, the whole line working capitally, and being much too clever for the Reading halves. Play had only lasted seven minutes when, from a long pass by Smith, **Copeland** scored a smart goal for the Hotspur, who from that point had a big share of the game.

Several times Reading were hard pressed, and Cameron hit the upright after a free kick. Following a couple of corners to Reading the home forwards ran down and, from a centre by Smith, **Brown** scored a second goal. During the next quarter of an hour Reading held their own, and ends were changed with the score two to none against them.

The Hotspur at once settled down again on the game being resumed, and admirable passing begun by Morris and continued by Cameron, Kirwan and Copeland ended in **Brown** shooting a goal. This was seven minutes after restarting, and, with a lead of three goals, the Tottenham players had the game well in hand. After a time they relaxed their efforts somewhat, but Tait and Erentz defended steadily. Towards the close the play became uninteresting, Reading failing in their attempts to reduce the lead against them. Very cold weather prevailed, but the conditions were quite favourable to the game, which attracted a crowd of 12,000 people. Now that Tottenham Hotspur have proved successful it is a remarkable fact that the four clubs badly favoured in the draw by having to play away from home have all qualified for the semi final ties, in which Tottenham Hotspur play West Bromwich Albion, and Sheffield United play Aston Villa. The grounds for the matches will be fixed tonight by the council.

RESULT: TOTTENHAM HOTSPUR 3 – READING 0

TOTTENHAM: Clawley (goal); Erentz and Tait (backs); Morris, Hughes and Jones (halves); Smith, Cameron, Brown [2], Copeland [1] and Kirwan (forwards).
READING: Cotton (goal); Henderson and Clinch (backs); Bull, Mainman and Watts (halves); Evans, Logan, Pegg, Barnes and A. Sharp (forwards).
Referee: Mr. A. Green (West Bromwich).

WOLVERHAMPTON WANDERERS v. SHEFFIELD UNITED
Third Round Proper – Saturday 25th March, 1901
Athletic News - Monday 25th February, 1901
A BIG VICTORY FOR SHEFFIELD UNITED.
[By the Free Critic.]

What with the circumscribed nature of the Small Heath ground, and the absence of West Bromwich, not to mention the attractiveness of the Sheffield United team, there was bound to be a big attendance at Wolverhampton. I don't know how far the Black Country extends, but, judging from the number of vehicles of various descriptions which were driven into the town, I should say the districts outside Wolverhampton were pretty well emptied so far as the male population was concerned. I was told that there had been a continuous procession from one o'clock, but there was no particular need to hurry, for there is any amount of room at Molineux, and although nearly 27,000 paid for admission, a few more thousands could have been provided for. The day was an ideal one for tootball - scarcely any breeze, but sufficiently cold to cause you to prefer football to cricket, and the huge embankment on the town side of the ground looked very fine and large with tier after tier of spectators. Many old faces were seen around the enclosure, and two well-known Internationals in Charlie Mason and W. I. Bassett were comparing notes. I was pleased to see Mr. T. H. Sidney once more out and about, for he had a severe dose of home confinement, and was probably more concerned about the compulsory if temporary retirement from the game both as a spectator and as a legislator. Then a very old League colleague in Mr. Allt was as keenly interested as ever, and the members of the F.A. Selection Committee were in attendance previous to completing their not very easy task of picking a team to beat Scotland next Saturday.

SHEFFIELD TO THE FORE

From the very kick-off it was pretty evident we had to have a real Cup-tie - no begging pardon if you happened to send an opponent flying, or considering his feelings in the slightest degree. And yet, with but few exceptions. there was nothing vicious about it, and no one seemed to raise serious objections. Mr. Kingscott, the referee, kept his weather eye open, and handled the game very well indeed. The United were not long in showing that they meant business, and once on the wing they went straight ahead, and generally contrived to finish in the immediate vicinity of Baddeley. The home forwards had not the same method in their movements, and I might also add that their backs were not of the robust character of those belonging to Sheffield United. The first goal came from a shocking bit of play on the part of Barker, who let in Priest, and had no earthly chance with the shot. The Wolves were by no means discouraged at this reverse, and when Mr. Kingscott awarded them a penalty for the United playing two goalkeepers, a big shout went up. But Harper aimed most accurately at the massive Foulke, and the opportunity was lost. The United did the bulk of the pressing, but the Wolves often enough got away, and once the ball was put through, but off-side was allowed. Then Miller, who had made some speedy and telling runs on the outside left, put in a centre right off the line, and the ball kept within a few inches of it all the way, Bowen completely missing it clean in front of goal. This was about the nearest thing the Wolves had during the afternoon. Directly afterwards the United had entered the semi-final, for in the short space of five minutes Hedley, Priest, and Bennett had each scored. The first was put across by Lipsham to Bennett, returned to Lipsham, who transferred it to **Hedley**, and No. 2 was registered. The next was the most beautifully worked goal of the lot. Priest giving the ball back to Needham, who passed on to Lipsham, the young Crewe man returning it to his partner, who dashed it across to Bennett, and the latter centred to **Priest**, not one of the Wolves touching it so far as I saw. Lipsham and Bennett had the next pretty much to themselves, **Bennett** ultimately heading past Baddeley. All this occurred with such rapidity that the spectators could scarcely realise it, and before they had time to recover, the whistle blew for the interval, the United leading by four to none.

A BARREN HALF

The Wolves made a better fight of it in the second half, although Baddeley had probably quite as much to do, for the United forwards, once within range, and sometimes before, were continually shooting and shooting hard. But the Wolves found Foulke most work, and certainly deserved to score at least one goal, for they strove hard against tremendous odds, and without the slightest possibility of winning. But they were dreadfully poor in front of goal - that is, in finishing, and evidently had designs on the crowd half way up the hill. Still Foulke had more than one awkward shot, and even the disappointed spectators found time to laugh heartily when Wooldridge caught Foulke with one foot off the ground and rolled him over, but the next moment the giant had his revenge by deliberately running up the line to charge Wooldridge. Needless to say the Wolverhampton forward fell. The game continued with the Wolves striving all the way to the very end, but Sheffield quite held their own, and entered the next round with a big victory of lour goals to none.

THE BETTER SIDE WON

There was no question of Sheffield United's superiority - it was too marked not to be distinctly visible to the most blindly enthusiastic follower of the "Wolves" - and yet there were occasions when the home side might possibly have had a chance, for you can hardly estimate the value of a goal in a Cup-tie, and had that penalty been successful, or had Bowen caught that beautiful centre of Miller's, things might have been different. Mind you, I don't think these incidents affected the ultimate result, for the United played such a storming game in the first halt that they would have beaten any team. And then look at the moral effect of scoring those three goals in five minutes just before the interval, when the United retired with light hearts, while the "Wolves" were naturally dejected during their brief rest! The one thing I admired in the "Wolves" was their pluck in the second half, when playing against such formidable score, but I can easily understand them losing matches if their forwards go about their work in such an unmethodical manner as on Saturday.

THE VANQUISHED

Wolverhampton have never been noted for really class forwards, but they were always the go-ahead type, and when they got near goal they had a shy and likewise a rush in the case of accidents. The present team, to my mind, attempts to be too clever without the necessary ability, and if they had only gone straight for goal, instead of endeavouring to work for openings which the I defence did not allow them to secure, they would have done much better. All the same, I would like them to have scored a legitimate point, if only as a reward for their persistent pertinacity. Bowen, on the extreme right, is very speedy, but lacks experience and does not centre at the right moment. As Bassett remarked when Lipsham and Bennett were passing with superb accuracy, "That is what you require in a Cup tie - give your other wing a chance." Well, Bassett ought to know, for he has won the English Cup and at least one Scotland match by it. Beats was disappointing, and tried to do too much, and I should say Miller was the best forward, especially in the first half. The middle line was not good so far as attack was concerned, except in making returns which might have meant goals had forwards been in a position to utilise them. But the halves seldom gave those in front of them a real chance, and forwards cannot play a proper game unless their halves feed them. The backs were risky. That is to say, they never struck you as being safe, for they didn't work together, and when they got the ball away you heaved a sigh of relief, for you were not at all certain in what direction it would go. I don't blame Baddely, although he ought to have stopped one goal, and in the second half was nearly rushed through with the ball in his possession, but he made some fine clearances, and had not the slightest chance with three of the four shots which scored.

THE VICTORS

On Saturday's form the United have a team capable of winning the Cup. There is no fiddling about. The backs kick for all they are worth; the halves recognise the fact that they are behind some forwards whom they keep continually on the move, and the front line does not hang on the ball, but gets it away, and there is generally someone ready to take it along. I know it is a mere detail, but they also have Ernest Needham as captain. Foulke is as big and as nimble as ever, and little fault could found with the two backs, who were tearless, if a little rash. Needham might with advantage look after his own side of the field, but is such a ubiquitous beggar that he seems able to fill the places of two or three men. Morren is not nearly so good as he was, and ought to know by this time that the Rugby Union laws as to collaring an opponent are not generally recognised in Association circles. Lipsham pleased me best of the forwards, and rarely made a mistake either in centring or passing, and another season should see this young man at the top of the tree. He never seemed to unduly exert himself, but was always there, and the ball invariably left his toe to one of his own side. Priest fed him well, and is a clever inside left, whilst with professionals on either side of him I should say Hedley is the best centre we have. Not much was seen of Field, but he gave Bennett any number of opportunities, and the inside right did not fail to utilise them with the well-timed centres and shots at goal.

RESULT: WOLVERHAMPTON WANDERS 0 - SHEFFIELD UNITED 4

SHEFFIELD UTD: Foulke (goal); Thickett and Wood (backs); Johnson, Morren and Needham (halves); Bennet [1], Field, Hedley [1], Priest [2] and Lipsham (forwards).
WOLVERHAMPTON W.: Baddeley (goal); Barker and Davies (backs); Annis, Pheasant and Fleming (halves); Bowen, Harper, Beats, Wooldridge and Miller (forwards).
Referee: anon ()

F.A. CUP - SEMI-FINALS

'Spurs tie against West Bromwich Albion at Villa Park was the first Semi-Final in the almost thirty year history of the competition to be scheduled to take place on any day other than a Saturday. This had been brought about by the passing of Queen Victoria in January, at which time football had been temporarily suspended whilst the nation was in mourning, thus throwing the schedules into chaos.

For the 'Spurs it was likely to be their toughest test in the competition so far. Athough the Albion were rooted to the foot of the First Division and looking certain for relegation, they were still, at that moment a First Division side, and one with a formidable cup pedigree. Moreover, the selection of Villa Park as the venue for the tie was very much in Albion's favour, being practically on their doorstep.

TOTTENHAM HOTSPUR v. WEST BROMWICH ALBION
Semi-Final – Monday 8th April, 1901
at Villa Park, Birmingham
The Sportsman - Tuesday 9th April, 1901
THE SPURS WIN EASILY - BROWN SCORES ALL FOUR GOALS.

It is a grievous pity that such a fine organisation as the Aston Villa F.C. cannot come to terms with the Post Office authorities in respect of the telegraphic facilities. Pressmen at the big match yesterday had to send each message on a good two mile journey before reaching the wires, and this state of affairs which ought not to prevail upon such important occasions. In all other respects the great match has to be pronounced a striking success. The holding capacity of the Villa ground was taxed to the uttermost, but there were few grumblings on the score of a bad view, while those in charge had the good sense to refuse admission to the cheaper part when the crush began to be severe. The result of the game was a crushing defeat for the Albion by four goals to love, and the manner in which the 'Spurs emphasised their superiority came as a great surprise to a large majority of Midland sportsmen. It really seems as if the old order of things in cup-ties is to be reversed, for once again the Tottenham players found cohesive principles and pretty methods all round more than a match for the rough and tumble and unscientific football with which West Bromwich Albion and other famous cup teams have made big reputations. When eleven men all pull one way, as the Spurs did yesterday, it is very difficult to signal out any particular one for an extra meed of praise. Possibly Tottonians will delight in regarding Brown as the hero of the match, and it must be said that the centre forward made the most of his opportunities. Brown may not be an ideal centre, but he has a keen eye to the main chance, and discriminates nicely as to when to score with the head, and when with the foot. His third goal - all were scored in the second half - was a magnificent effort from thirty yards out. He headed another from a cross by N. Irwin, also scored from a nicely-placed corner, while he wound up with a fourth as the outcome of a pretty passing run. It will thus be seen that Brown was finely supported by his colleagues, and this very pronounced unselfishness was one of the features of Tottenham's display. Kirwan played a great game on the extreme left, and nothing could have been finer than the centre from close on the touch line which led to the scoring the first goal. Cameron, as usual, worked like a Trojan, and was often very effective when dropping back to help the halves. Smith appeared to be excited at the start, but he improved wonderfully, although he was not favoured by the chances that fell to the left wing. Copeland contented himself by nursing Kirwan, and fulfilled his task in a highly satisfactory manner. All three halves were quick to pounce on the ball, but the honours in this department undoubtedly went to Hughes, who was all over Stevenson, and then had time to spare for other duties. As a matter of fact, Hughes was a long way the best half on the field, and played his most successful game of the Cup-tie series. Tait was in rare fettle at back, and always inspired confidence, while the tall kicking and fine tackling of Erentz was equally as effective, though not so polished. Occasionally Clawley was hard pressed, and he distinguished himself chiefly by the finished manner in which he dealt with high shots and prevented scores from corner kicks. It must be confessed that the Albion disappointed their friends by their lack of mutual understanding. Vigour and determination were not wanting, but their forwards quite failed to get together. Kick and rush was the order, and against a less solid defence these tactics might have paid. Occasionally Wheldon - scarcely the Wheldon of old - would send across a finely-judged pass, but little would be made of it. Possibly the want of success in the front line was in a measure due to the erratic kicking of the halves, of whom Hadley was the most energetic. Adams and Dunn, had a hard afternoon's work at back, and on the whole did well. They had the common fault of the team, however, that of recklessness. The poor goal record of the Albion assuredly largely due to the lack support the forwards received from the rear division, for it was not very often yesterday that the front line had a good opening made for it. No blame attaches to Reader for the downfall of his side, the old stager practically having no chance with any of Brown's efforts. In a sense the Albion should be thankful for their defeat, if not the severity of it, for they can now assiduously apply themselves to the task of escaping relegation the Second League. So far as Tottenham are concerned, they improved as the game went on. For the first quarter of an hour they failed to take the measure of a worrying and vigorous defence, but afterwards were all over the better side. Before the first portion was out, the visitors seemed to have taken half the vast crowd on their side, and it really must be said that the spectators were most sportsmanlike, and impartially cheered good play.

When the interval arrived, nothing had been scored, but five minutes after resuming Hughes passed to Kirwan and Kirwan to **Brown**, the latter heading through from close quarters. Tottenham never looked like losing from this point, and eleven minutes later Jones, of the Albion, thought fit to give Brown a hug, and following the free kick Cameron forced a corner, from which **Brown** scored number two. Three minutes after this **Brown** was enthusiastically cheered for a lovely shot from long range, which beat Reader all ends up, and this practically decided the issue. For about ten minutes the Albion tried hard, and secured several corners, and was here that Clawley came in so useful, but ten minutes had to go when Smith careered away after receiving from Cameron. The right-winger sent a nice pass across to **Brown**, and Reader was beaten for the fourth and last time, Tottenham thus qualifying for the final in very handsome fashion, and fully bearing out the predictions in yesterday's Sportsman. Come Sheffield United, come Aston Villa, the fight at the Crystal Palace on the 20th inst. will be a great one, for the 'Spurs have proved themselves to be a team worthy of the highest honours, and with just a chance of winning the Association Cup. The teams yesterday were precisely as advertised, except that Wheldon came in the Albion front line for Buck, and played inside right, Smith crossing over. At the close of the game, which was watched 45,000 people, the gate receipts amounting to £1852. Brown collared the ball, which he intends to keep as a memento of a big occasion.

RESULT: TOTTENHAM HOTSPUR 4 – WEST BROMWICH ALBION 0

TOTTENHAM: Clawley (goal); Erentz and Tait (backs); Morris, Hughes and Jones (halves); Smith, Cameron, Brown [4], Copeland and Kirwan (forwards).
WEST BROMWICH: Reader (goal); Adams and Dunn (backs); Perry, Jones and Hadley (halves); Roberts, Wheldon, Stevenson, Smith and Walker (forwards).
Referee: Mr. J. Lewis (Blackburn).

SHEFFIELD UNITED v. ASTON VILLA
Semi-Final – Saturday 6th April, 1901
at The City Ground, Nottingham
The Sportsman - Tuesday 9th April, 1901

Thirty thousand people at the City Ground, Nottingham on Saturday witnessed the contest between Aston Villa and Sheffield United in the semi-final round of the Association Cup. The ground of the Forest Club is well known to both teams, and each has a strong contingent of admirers locally, so that, being within easy railway journey of both Sheffield and Birmingham, no venue could have been more suitable. The arrangements made by the officials both of the Notts Association and of the Forest Club were very satisfactory, and the post-office dealt expeditiously with considerable quantity of telegraphing. Poorly as the morning promised, the day turned out very warm and fine, and football was witnessed under very pleasant conditions. The teams had been well trained for the event, the Sheffield men at Skegness, and the Villa players at Droitwich and Blackpool. Neither club could put the best reputed eleven into the field, for on the Sheffield side, although Boyle was able to play, Thickett was out, owing to the death of his young wife; whilst on the Villa side Johnson and Spencer were absentees through injuries. It was shortly after half-past three when Hedley started the ball for Sheffield United, who lost toss, and who played against an oblique wind. They started at a tremendous rate, and for quite 20 minutes the spectators were treated to a series hot attacks on the Villa goal, made with all the go and energy of the days when the "Sheffield rush" was a thing to fear. The Villa defence was not very steady to start with, but the Sheffielders were in a desperate hurry to shoot, and made erratic use of some very apparent chances. Twice Templeton removed the ball to the other end of the field, but the United could not be kept out, and ere the game was five minutes old Priest scored from a rebound off Evans, who had intercepted a centre from Lipsham. The excited spectators followed the game after this with cheers and counter-cheers, but the advantage of attack was with Sheffield. Templeton, who lay well up, was fed by Athersmith and Devey, and, though the right wing of the Villa as a combination was poor, Templeton was often in evidence for smart runs. Needham took the duty of looking after Athersmith, and left Boyle the task of taking Templeton's centres, with the result that, although there often seemed danger to the United goal, Foulke was hardly called upon at all in the first half hour. The game had been in progress 55 minutes, when Garratty, a very speedy left, got away by himself, and, going too fast for Beers, shot into the Sheffield net from about twelve yards distance, Foulke having no chance. The United were stimulated by the reverse, and the scores did not long remain equal, for just before the end of the first half Bennett got in one of the very few centres Wilkes had allowed him to and the ball was eventually left for Lipsham to score a cool and admirably-shot goal, but not a credit to the Villa defence, for Lipsham was left entirely uncovered. Thus Sheffield crossed over leaders by two goals to one, having set the pace from the start, but playing less accurately than the Villa team.

The second half saw the Villa taking the lead in point of play, for Templeton was utilised to the full, and from one of his centres the ball was headed past Foulke, Garratty and Devey doing the trick between them. Play had proceeded barely six minutes when this happened, and no other goal was afterwards obtained; but for quite half an hour the most strenuous onslaughts were made by both sides. Lipsham had been badly kicked in the ribs, accidentally, by Crabtree, and in the second half was not of much service, whilst towards the close the Sheffielders lost Field, who got a blow on the ankle from Wilkes and had to go off. Still there were times when the Villa looked looked like being beaten. Had Templeton, however, had strength to shoot hard in finishing at least two of his brilliant runs, there would have been no need to replay the game. The contest was fought on fairly good-tempered lines, though Crabtree, Cowan and Hedley were each penalised, as was Athertsmith for fouling Foulke. It was, however, a fine game, in which the Villa forwards showed excellent passing, the Sheffielders great dash, whilst the defence on both sides was very good, the Sheffield halves particularly so. The "gate" was £1500.

RESULT: SHEFFIELD UNITED 2 – ASTON VILLA 2

SHEFFIELD UTD: Foulke (goal); Beers and Boyle (backs); Johnson, Morren and Needham (halves); Bennet, Field, Hedley, Lipsham [1] and Priest [1] (forwards).
ASTON VILLA: George (goal); Crabtree and Evans (backs); Bowman, Cowan and Wilkes (halves); Templeton, Athersmith, Devey [1], Garratty [1] and Smith (forwards).
Referee: Mr. A. G. Kingscott (Derby)

SHEFFIELD UNITED v. ASTON VILLA
Semi-Final (Replay) – Thursday 11th April, 1901
at Baseball Ground, Derby
London Evening Standard - Friday 12th April, 1901

Having played a drawn game of two goals each at Nottingham, on Saturday last, these teams met again yesterday on the ground of the Derby Football Club, when the Sheffielders, giving a grand display, in marked contrast to their exhibition at the previous meeting, gained a brilliant and well-deserved victory by three goals to none. The match was favoured with fine, if somewhat dull, weather, and with the special trains from Sheffield and Birmingham well patronised, the attendance numbered 22,200, the gate receipts being £997. Both clubs made changes from the teams that had taken part in the previous game at Nottingham. On the Sheffield side, Thickett resumed his place at full back, whilst Almond took the place of Field in the front rank.

Cowans injury prevented him turning out for the Villa, and Wilkes had to be moved to centre half, whilst Noon was introduced to the right half position. It was a few minutes after four o'clock when the game started, and for the first twenty minutes an exhibition of football was given that was singularly interesting. The Sheffielders, who had won the toss, were sided by what wind there was, and were kicking towards the Barracks goal. Some fine work by Needham at once placed the Villa goal in jeopardy. He passed forward, and George ran out and saved in time. Lipsham was very active on the Sheffield side at this point, and once he secured the ball in splendid fashion, the ball skimming the cross-bar. He repeated the performance shortly afterwards, and on that occasion George turned the ball over the bar. The corner that resulted brought a second, but neither of them were turned to account. The Villa were sometime ere they got away, but at last Templeton tricked Needham, and put the ball across to Athersmith, who compelled Foulke to save. Devey also called upon the big man, but play was soon at the other end again, and George had to clear a couple of corners. Bennett appeared to get clear away, and be looked certain to score, but the United's supporters were doomed to disappointment. They were at length rewarded, however, as, after twenty-five minutes, the ball was sent up the field by Boyle, and Bennett, taking advantage of a mistake by Noon, went through and scored a capital goal, the ball striking the inside of the post in its progress into the net. This success of the Yorkshiremen was hailed with tumultuous cheering, and from now to the interval the Villa did not make very strenuous efforts to rob them of their lead: the football fell off in point interest, and half-time found the score still unaltered.

For some time after change of ends the Villa pressed, but it cannot be said that there was a great deal of sting about their efforts. The Sheffield backs and halves were playing grandly, and though Foulke's goalkeeping was not quite so clean as it might have been, the Villa can hardly be said to have looked like scoring. After a while Sheffield opened out splendidly, and for the last twenty minutes of the game their superiority was most marked. Aided by a clever pass from Hedley, Priest obtained possession in a dangerous position, and refusing to be baffled by the pressing attentions of the Villa backs, went through and scored. This was 17 minutes from the close, and may said to have destroyed the last vestige of interest in the game, for the United were now exhibiting such an amount of cleverness, and were playing so well within themselves, that it was obvious to everyone that nothing could prevent the Villa being beaten, However, seven minutes from the close. Priest effectually settled matters by scoring a third and equally brilliant goal.

RESULT: SHEFFIELD UNITED 3 – ASTON VILLA 0

SHEFFIELD UTD: Foulke (goal); Thickett and Boyle (backs); Johnson, Morren and Needham (halves); Bennet [1], Almond, Hedley, Priest [2] and Lipsham (forwards).
ASTON VILLA: George (goal); Crabtree and Evans (backs); Noon, Wilkes and Bowman (halves); Templeton, Athersmith, Devey, Garratty and Smith (forwards).
Referee: Mr. A. G. Kingscott (Derby)

F.A. CUP - THE FINAL

Bios on following pages either from 'Lancashire Daily Post' 20/04/1901, or 'Sporting Life' 20/04/1901. Team images above from 'Sporting Life'.

PLAYER COMPARISONS

	TOTTENHAM HOTSPUR							SHEFFIELD UNITED			
NAME	Nat.	Ht	Wt.	AGE	POS.	AGE	Wt.	Ht.	Nat.	NAME
Clawley	EN	6'1"	12/7	25	GK	26	19/10	6'2"	EN	Foulke
Erentz	SC	5'11"	12/10	24	RB	29	11/7	5'10"	EN	Thickett
Tait	SC	5'9½"	11/10	29	LB	25	12/7	5'10½"	IR	Boyle
Morris	EN	5'9"	11/12	24	RH	29	10/9	5'5"	EN	Needham
Hughes	WL	5'8"	11/7	24	CH	27	10/7	5'5½"	EN	Morren
Jones	WL	5'10"	12/8	30	LH	25	11/4	5'8"	EN	Johnson
Smith	EN	5'7½"	11/4	26	OR	26	11/9	5'7"	EN	Bennett
Cameron	SC	5'10"	11/6	28	IR	23	10/7	5'6"	EN	Field
Brown	SC	5'10"	11/6	23	CF	25	11/7	5'10"	EN	Hedley
Copeland	SC	5'7"	11/6	25	IL	28	11/7	5'8"	EN	Priest
Kirwan	IR	5'6½"	10/8	23	OL	22	11/0	5'8"	EN	Lipsham
Totals		63'6½"	128/4	281		288	141/10	63'3"		Totals
Averages		5'9"	11/10	25.5		26.1	12/14	5'9"		Averages

(Heights in feet ' and inches ", Weights in stones/pounds)

As can be seen from the table above, the teams were very evenly matched in terms of age and height.

At first glance Sheffield United appear to have a significant weight advantage of over 1 stone (6.3 kilos) per man. In fact this figure is grossly distorted by United's supersized keeper, Willie Foulke. Calculated without Foulke, the average weight of the United players, at 11st. 3lb., is actually less than that of the 'Spurs men!

Preparing for the Final

Sheffield United prepared for the final by spending a week in training on the sands at Skegness, being quartered at the Sea View Hotel. With several of the team suffering minor ailments the training duties were kept generally light, consisting of light exercise and sprinting for the outfielders and Indian clubs for Foulke. All the players responded well so that by Friday, when the team left for Sydenham, all were reported to be available for selection.

Training qurater's for the 'Spurs team was at the Royal Forest Hotel in Chingford where relaxation was more the order of the day. After training in the morning, which again mostly consisted of light sprinting, the players were left to their own desires in the afternoons, which most spent playing golf or taking peaceful walks in the forest. The evenings then being spent at billiards or whist.

THE GOALKEEPERS

GEORGE CLAWLEY, the Tottenham goalkeeper, is one of the three total abstainers of the team. standing six feet high, and blessed with any amount of agility, he is extremely hard to beat, and the 'Spurs last line of defence has been in safe keeping since the Stoke man was secured a few years ago. Clawley has also worn the Southampton colours, and though hardly equal in brilliance to Sutcliffe, Robinson, or McBride, he is yet a very safe custodian.

WILLIAM FOULKE or "Little Willie" as he is familiarly termed by Sheffield sportsmen, is a most interesting personage in English football. With a height of 6ft. 2in., he boasts of adipose tissue, &c., to the extent of 21st., but, considering his weight, he is astonishingly nimble and active, and woe betide the forward who endeavours to force him into the net. Foulke is a native of Derbyshire, and has earned some distinction in cricket circles, representing his country in a number of engagements last summer. He is seldom beaten with a high shot, but finds those below the level of the knees most difficult to cope with. He can land a ball as far as with his fist as some men can do with their feet.

THE RIGHT BACKS

The Newton Heath officials were very loth to part with **HARRY ERENTZ**, when the latter decided to cast in his lot with a Southern organisation, and migrated to Tottenham, for he had shown excellent defence during his brief connection with the team. Prior to joining the Manchester club he played with a Lancashire League organisation, but he is a Scotchman by birth, and learned the rudiments of the game at Dundee.

HARRY THICKETT, the right full back, has rendered valiant service for the United for the United for a number of seasons. His burly frame enables him to "rush" opposing forwards in a manner peculiar to himself, and when in form he is decidedly difficult to pass. He possesses a fair turn of speed, uses his head well, and possesses a good variety of kicks. A native of Rotherham, he soon came to the fore, and has been capped upon more than one occasion

LEFT BACKS

ALEXANDER TAIT, "Sandy", as he is familiarly called, is well known. His grit, determination, and resourceful back play made him a big favourite with Deepdale crowds, for no matter whether the occasion was an important League game or a Lancashire Combination fixture, in which the North End held a substantial lead, Sandy would play the same hard, vigorous game, and leave nothing to chance. He is a native of Ayrshire, but whilst in Preston he married a Prestonian, and has a close connection with the town. A dispute as to terms was responsible for his departure from Preston, and whilst the North End and Notts Forest officials were coming to an arrangement as to a transfer, the Tottenham secretary slipped in and made a smart capture.

PETER BOYLE was hardly an unqualified success when he was transferred from Sunderland three years ago and came to Sheffield to fill the post vacated by Cain. However, upon getting into his stride he quickly established himself a favourite with the crowd and has done considerably good work in the United defence. He makes an admirable partner for Thickett.

RIGHT HALVES

EDWARD HUGHES is the right hand member of a very evenly balanced half-back line, there being little to choose between the trio. He can also play at left half, and, like his club mate, Jones, has represented the Leek against the Rose, Thistle and the Shamrocks. A clever tackler and an expert feeder, Hughes infuses plenty of dash into his work, and possesses the happy knack of getting his forwards going. He played with Everton for several seasons.

The United's midget intermediate line – broken somewhat by the departure of Rab Howell for Liverpool two years ago – has always been a strong one. **HARRY JOHNSON**, the latest arrival in the half-back line, is the light-weight of the team, turning the scale at 10½ stone. A local lad, he has improved wonderfully since his introduction to First League football. No doubt he has learned a wrinkle or two from the play of Needham. He is an untiring worker.

CENTRE HALVES

TOM MORRISS is a member of the intermediate line, and is not, as his name would signify, a Welshman, for Lincolnshire was his birthplace. A glutton for work, and almost rivalling Sandy Tait in his fearlessness and determination, Morris proves a stumbling block to the majority of opposing forwards.

TOM MORREN looks a veritable midget compared with the comedian, but despite his small bulk he is a pacey, energetic, hard-working centre-half, and as clever an exponent of Socker as can be found in the kingdom. He joined the United from Middlesbrough and made his mark from the start, and he enters upon League and Cup-tie matches with a never say die sort of spirit. At Newcastle on Saturday he received a nasty blow in stopping a hot shot from Gardner, and did not recover consciousness until on the journey home. International honours have come his way.

LEFT HALVES

JOHN L. JONES is one of the veterans of the team. He has represented Wales in several international encounters with distinct success, and before casting in his lot with the 'Spurs, he played with Bootle, Stockton, and Sheffield United. A fair cricketer and a good all-round sportsman, the Welshman is, like Clawley, a teetotaller.

ERNEST NEEDHAM has earned such fame, and been portrayed by so many pens, that it is useless to descant on his wonderful abilities here. Suffice it to say that he is the finest all-round footballer in the world – a large but none the less truthful statement. Whether it be in defence, bottling up opposing inside men, or leading a furious attack on the opposite goal, Needham is seen at his best, and few forwards have proved themselves qualified to shine against him. He has played in every position in the field bar goal, and would doubtless appear between the sticks did opportunity arise, according to those who know him intimately, he is as tenacious as he is clever. Certainly he is the mainspring of the team.

OUTSIDE RIGHTS

TOM SMITH, No. 1, as he came to be styled in Preston when second Tom Smith appeared on the scene, is the flier of the eleven, and it will have gone hard with the United today if Needham did not get the measure of the speedy Maryport player, and keep him within bounds. Smith is one of the fastest men playing Association football, and has won quite a number of local sprints. At Preston he lacked elusive tactics, although a goodly number of goals resulted from his quick bursts and flying centres. Since migrating south, however, he has improved wonderfully in finesse and resource.

WALTER BENNETT joined the United from Mexborough, and, when a member of that now defunct team, shot goals as if they were sparrows. All Mexboro' now visits Bramall-lane to see him play. When at his best he deserves their patronage. Is very fast – faster than one would think to look at him - can shoot like the rush of a cannon ball, and almost as straight. Has scored some wonderful goals in his day, and still gets them, though they were not forthcoming in this year's internationals. Crabtree says "he hits the ball harder than any man in England". Received his caps this season v. Wales and Scotland.

INSIDE RIGHTS

JOHN CAMERON is one of the best fellows imaginable. Whether as player, club manager, secretary of the Players' Union, or as a private individual he is a pleasant companion; and perhaps the high degree of success the Hotspurs have attained is due in no small measure to the esteem in which he is held by the players and officials. From Queens Park he went to Liverpool, and played with Everton as an amateur, afterwards adopting football as a profession. Finding the Everton camp hardly to his liking, he joined the 'Spurs, and his knowledge of Northern and Midland first class football has enabled him to build up the present powerful team.

CHAS. FIELD, barring Lipsham, is the only member of the team who did not help to win the final tie against Derby County two years ago. Like nine other members of the eleven he is an Englishman, being born at Hanwell, London, 23 years ago. He has proved himself a useful inside forward, but in company with Lipsham, only comes into the cup team by reason of the absence of Beers and Almond.

CENTRE FORWARDS

ALEXANDER (Sandy) BROWN is another ex-North Ender. He has recently startled the football world by his remarkable sharpshooting in this season's English Cup Competition. It is not left to many centre forwards to score as many as 12 out of 15 goals obtained by a side in four ties, but this is what Sandy has accomplished for Tottenham. At Preston he showed marked ability, and at times an inclination to lose his temper. He was known in League circles as "the boy centre" for he was only 17 years of age when he came to Preston from Ayrshire.

GEORGE A. HEDLEY is another of the men who were spotted in Northern League days, comes from the Teeside. He was a hard man to get hold of as he preferred football as amateur to professional lines. He decided to accept the offer of the United, however. When first he joined the club he had all the arts and touches of a class player, and the Sheffield polish has been applied so assiduously that he this season gained his cap in the match of the season against Wales at Newcastle, a few weeks ago. He is a gentleman player and a general favourite.

INSIDE LEFTS

DAVID COPELAND popularly known as 'Davie', is a Scotchman to the backbone, and was born in Ayr. He is twenty four years old, First played for Ayr Parkhouse, whom he assisted to win the Ayr and Kilmarnock Charity Cups. Walsall's agents noted his play, and for four season he represented them at centre and inside positions. Whilst there the Villa and all the leading Midland clubs applied for his transfer but with no success. Smart at dribbling, and a rattling shot, who takes a lot of shifting off the ball, Davie is a player to be reckoned with.

FRED PRIEST, notwithstanding his penchant for getting injured, has few superiors as an outside left. With a rare turn of speed and good command of the ball right across the goal-mouth with unerring accuracy from the very corner. and is a steady plodding rather than a brilliant forward. He has hardly fulfilled the expectations formed of him at the outset of his career.

OUTSIDE LEFTS

JOHN KIRWAN is one of the cleverest of Irish footballers, Kirwan has been giving some brilliant displays for the 'Spurs this season. He was born at Wicklow, whence he migrated to Southport as a youngster. In the course of time his ability led to trouble between Blackburn Rovers and Everton, and finally the latter club paid £250 for his transfer. He is a natural footballer, and a player of the highest class, and last year played for Ireland against Wales.

BERT LIPSHAM came to the United from the Crewe Alexandra Club at the end of last season. It was notorious that he was sought after by several big League clubs, but the Sheffield one secured his services, and he had no reason to regret the substantial outlay his transfer cost. He plays on either wing – the best on the left, where his speed and cleverness are always telling. He is a brilliant centre, and shoots finely to best, whilst in dribbling he has no superiors. Indeed, such an impression did he make on the selection committee in the cup-tie at Wolverhampton that he was well in the running for his cap against Scotland. He was a very long time in getting his first goal for United, and this only came in the first round of this season's cup ties, but since then he has scored several fine goals for his new club.

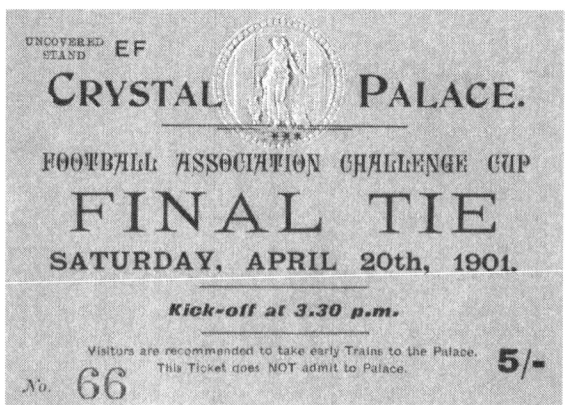

WITH THE TOTTENHAM MEN ON THE EVE OF THE BATTLE
Sheffield Daily Telegraph - Saturday 20 April 1901

One of our London representatives, writing yesterday, says:—

"I again visited Chingford this morning, and found the Tottenham men quietly awaiting the great event. Making the most of the brilliant sunshine, the men were in the open air, one or two of them taking a walk in the direction of Chingford Town. A few of the more boisterous spirits spent a merry half-hour outside the Forest Hotel riddling an old silk hat with missiles, whilst another member sat and "snap-shotted" them. The quiet life begun on Monday has been continued, and in order to avoid anything which might tend to undue excitement the directors at the last moment decided to abandon the proposed trip to the Stratford Empire Music Hall. I found that the entire team, without exception, are in excellent health, with the result it is now practically decided that the eleven which did duty at Birmingham against West Bromwich Albion will play to-morrow."

"As the contest draws nearer, the Tottenham men seem to grow in confidence as to the result. Smith, the ex-Preston North Ender, is especially cocksure. With the prospect of fine weather for the match, and consequent firm turf, he thinks the forwards will outrun their rivals. Having regard to the almost perfect condition of the team, he thinks firm ground will be a distinct advantage to his side. Tate and Clawley spoke with more reserve, but, notwithstanding, they think the 'Spurs will win. They recognise, however, that the United will exact from them their very best form. It must not be taken that the team as a whole are cocksure — in the extravagant interpretation of the word. The quiet confidence formerly spoken of still exists, with the possible difference that that feeling has perhaps grown a little stronger."

"As aforesaid, violent forms of exercise in training have been avoided. A little sprinting was indulged in this morning, and I was given to understand that each participant shaped well. So far as one could judge from appearance, every man looks in the pink of condition. Cameron returned to Tottenham for several hours to-day, being engaged on his secretarial duties. I ascertained that he is in form. Naturally, the men are getting very anxious, especially those whose nerves are more highly strung than those of their fellows."

"Up to the present the Tottenham men have received £36 a-piece in the way of bonuses, and I understand they are to have £25 a man if they bring off tomorrow's event, and £10 if they lose. I should mention that all the men consider that they showed their best form in the cup competition in their second match with Preston North End, at Deepdale. The 'Spurs leave Chingford Station to-morrow by the 11.55 train, by which they travel to Liverpool Street. Thence they complete their journey to the Palace by brake, where they expect to arrive somewhere about two o'clock."

TOTTENHAM'S CAPTAIN INTERVIEWED.

"We played our best game," said the captain of the 'Spurs yesterday to a Press representative, "against Preston and Bury, and though we have been rather loudly praised for our display at Birmingham, I do not think we quite merited it. If we have really merited all or any of the praise showered on us, it was for the games against the North End and Bury. The latter were a difficult nut to crack, but in both matches the play of our men was consistently good: at least we were not unequal, as against West Bromwich. In the first half at Birmingham our forwards were at sea, but our backs did well, and saved the situation. In the second half, on the other hand, the forwards did well. Our performance as a team was, however, unequal."

"To what do you attribute your success?"

"Mainly to our playing a cool and collected game, and to our not suffering ourselves to be influenced by the greatness of the occasion. The change of air and the quiet, regular life we lead at Chingford have helped to foster this coolness and ability to enter into a Cup tie..."

"Even the final?"

"Yes, even the final — as if it were a League or even an ordinary game. We believe in playing a winning game."

"Where does the strength of the team lie?"

"Our strength does not lie any particular department, but in an all-round, level of excellence, and in our combination and opportunism. We know each other's play nicely, and the team were never better together than at present. Some of the men, Cameron and Kirwan, for example, are brilliant individually as well collectively, and can on occasion use their special powers, while there is no better shot than Brown. We all feel well and fit, and feel somehow that we will 'bring it off.' Not a single man is in any sense on the injured list, and we have no 'crocks' liable to break down. I feel that we will win; in any case, we will play to win."

"What about the record crowd? Will 100,000 pairs of eyes, or 100,000 throats all shouting once, make difference?"

"Not a bit," said the skipper, with a smile, and twinkle in his eye; "we are used to big crowds now, and forget their presence when once the game is in full swing. I suppose we are case-hardened; in any case, I am, and it has been our aim to steer clear of Cup tie fever."

TOTTENHAM HOTSPUR v. SHEFFIELD UNITED
F.A. Cup Final – Saturday 20th April, 1901
at Crystal Palace, London
Athletic News - Monday 22nd April, 1901

SIDE LIGHTS ON THE GAME AND A FEW ODDS AND ENDS
[By Nondescript]

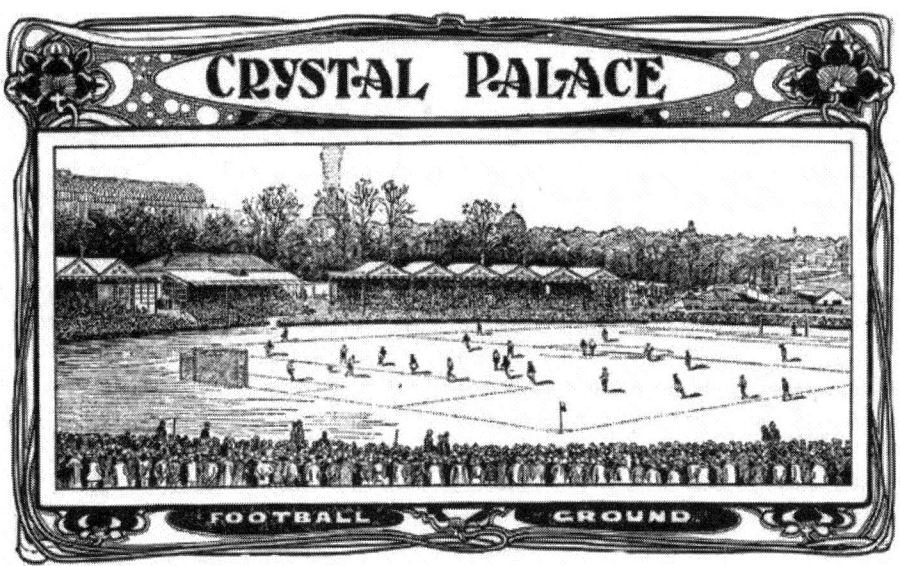

The final tie for the Football Association Cup has been singularly favoured so far as weather is concerned, for seldom indeed have we experienced anything but the most genial climatic conditions. At one period of last week, it almost seemed as if the event would be ruined, for from some cause or another the Crystal Palace ground has not turned out exactly to calculation in the matter of drainage, and we had ample evidence of the defect when the Sheriff of London Shield tie was played as well as in the International with Scotland a few weeks ago. It was a rather serious question, but was not unexpected, for the water from the Palace itself must go down the hill, and probably familiar associations decided it's next exact venue, for the present football ground was six years ago a lake, and at that time little if any objection could be taken to the influx of water. Now matters are much different, and it is really a serious matter,for on Wednesday, I am told, the ground was under water, but on Saturday Dr. W. G. Grace, who had carefully examined the turf, said it was all right, allowing for a

few very hard and a few very soft places. But what a glorious day it was! On Friday the chamberlain at the Tavistock Hotel aroused me with the information that it was a beautiful morning, and that it looked well for the final. He was quite right, for we seemed suddenly to have gone from winter to summer, and when one went out into the Strand it was to find the shop windows covered in sunshades, and straw hats appear on sale. There was a lot of legislative work to transact as is usual on the eve of the final, but never have I known so much interest to be taken in the match itself. The reason is not far to seek, for it is so many years since a London team appeared in the final stage. Certainly, last year Southampton were there, but Southampton, although a very important town, is not London. The porters in Covent Garden were continually referring to it, and many were the excited arguments I heard, for not a small number of the gentlemen who parade with pineapples their heads are provincials, and they don't seem ashamed to own it. If you called on a serious looking tobacconist for a modest couple of ounces, he was certain to ask you what you thought of the match, while the tonsorial artist who attended to requirements was most inquisitive. The 'bus drivers were also anxious for information, whilst if you took a hansom, the polite gentleman in charge was certain to ask your opinion whether the "Spurs" would win. Yes, London decidedly interested itself in the match, and, personally, I was very pleased to see it. Saturday morning was beautifully fine, and acting upon experience, we engaged a brake. It was a good job we did, for I am told that, admirable as were the arrangements made by the railway companies, it was a terrible struggle, and one friend of mine, who had worked out a quiet but circuitous route, spent three hours in his journey to the Palace. Yes, the best means of getting there is to drive, for not only do you really save time, but it is pleasant journey. Once inside the Palace and you are right, provided you have taken the precaution to get a ticket; otherwise you must rough it, and many thousands had to rough it on Saturday. When we reached the pavilion it was easy to see that the crowd would be a fine one, for an hour before the time of kick-off people had commenced to congregate in hundreds on the slopes outside the ground itself. They had only a partial view of the game, but didn't seem at all dissatisfied. On the contrary they were very jolly. To anyone who has been in the habit of witnessing finals at the Palace it was clearly evident that all records would be broken, for the flat spaces round the ropes were packed, and I was not surprised to hear that over 110,000 had paid for admission. I happened to be chatting with Dr. Grace when Lord Kinnaird arrived along with Sir Redvers Buller. Lady Audrey Buller, and Miss Buller, and had the extreme pleasure of a private introduction to the distinguished party, which was most heartily received. What a splendid full back Sir Redvers Buller would have made! That determined countenance and ponderous build of his would hare struck terror into the heart of an opposing forward. The teams turned out very punctually, and were exactly as reported.

THE GAME

The game has been variously described a good one, an indifferent one, an excellent one, an exciting one, and a poor one. Well, I have witnessed a good many finals, and never expect to see the best of football, but I can honestly say I have come across a great many worse than that of Saturday. There is no necessity to go into detail, but the first half was as good and exciting as it was possible to wish for, and under the broiling sun it was only natural that the players should slacken down, for however well trained they may be, the excitement – and on Saturday the heat - is more than they can stand for an hour and a half. It is held by many people that a professional footballer ought not to be affected by the surroundings; but he is and how can you wonder it with a hundred thousand pairs of eyes greedily devouring his every movement? In the old days at the Oval, although the interest was just as keen, and considering the numbers present, the shouting more robust, still, the number was limited, and no matter how stoical and self-possessed a player may be, he is bound to feel a touch of the excitement which permeates the thousands who have come to see him play. It was not particularly noticeable in the first half, which was as fast and as interesting and exciting as anyone would care to see, but it was in the second portion, when both sides were guilty of wild, indiscriminate kicking, which went for nothing at all. The United scored after ten minutes' play, the ever-obliging Priest doing the needful, but this did not prevent the 'Spurs playing up, and a miskick by Thickett, followed by a goal, resulted in **Brown** equalising from the free-kick admirably placed by the Tottenham captain. Brown must surely be the record scorer in the Cup Competition. The scene when Tottenham obtained that goal was the finest I have witnessed, and I am afraid many good, serviceable hats were lost for ever. It did one good to listen to the enthusiastic outbursts. Nothing further was done in the way of scoring up to the interval, so that the teams turned round with a goal apiece.

THE SECOND HALF

The second half opened sensationally, for the game had not been in progress many minutes when another huge shout - I wish I could find a more appropriate name for the cheering - announced the fact that Tottenham were ahead {*Brown*}. Their joy was, however, short-lived, for in about a minute Lipsham centred, and one of the United players banged the ball hard at Clawley from very short range. Clawley partially intercepted it, and sent it out, only to have it returned, whilst in the meantime the referee had pointed to the centre. The decision did not give general satisfaction, but Mr. Kingscott was in a capital position to judge, and there was no necessity to appeal to the linesmen. He was convinced the ball was over the line when Clawley cleared, and consequently gave it a goal. There were afterwards many sarcastic shouts of "goal" when the ball passed yards over or wide of the posts, but I am standing by Mr. Kingscott, who refereed a difficult match very well indeed. Both these goals were obtained within six minutes of the restart, and the remainder of the game was decidedly quiet and somewhat uninteresting. Certainly each goal had near escapes, and both Foulke and Clawley must be congratulated upon the coolness and nerve they displayed in dealing with what may be termed unexpected shots, but on the whole the play could only be adequately described as wild, and neither custodian was beaten, so that, for the first time since 1886, a draw has been made in the final tie, the re-play being at Bolton on Saturday next. Sir Redvers Buller had come down with the intention of presenting the Cup and medals, but that pleasure was denied him. However, he made a nice little speech, which chiefly referred to the necessity of learning how to shoot. No doubt, the gallant General was alluding to pompoms and things, but a few of our leading footballers may beneficially study the art, for I consider it sadly neglected. Redvers had a most hearty reception, and one sang "For he's jolly good fellow" three times. The great soldier seemed very well pleased, and in company with Lord Kinnaird, Mr. J.C. Clegg, and others, afterwards visited the players in their dressing-rooms. I don't know whether came across Foulke, as I did, in a perfectly nude state, but if so I am certain he would want know the amount of his transfer fee for service in South

Africa or any other country with which we may not be upon "friendly" terms. Altogether it may be described an interesting match without rising to the scientific, and really one does not expect too much science in a final. Anyone who does is likely to be disappointed, and very much so.

A LITTLE CRITICISM

I think the draw of two goals each an admirable result to a singularly even game. There were occasions when first one side and then the other had an advantage, but the chances of scoring were pretty well divided, and a similar remark will apply to what is generally known as bad luck. Both sides ought to have scored more often than they did, but were prevented from doing so by good goalkeeping, and shall I say ineffective shooting. The one thing I admired in Tottenham was the business-like manner in which they got away. There was no dallying with the ball. If the outside-left found he could not get through he parted with it to the outside-right, and vice-versa; and generally it came off. In fact, the feeding of the extreme wings seemed to be a feature the Tottenham people, and it was not a bad one either. It reminded me very much of the Blackburn Olympic style of play when they first took the Cup from the South. Tottenham were fully justified, for in Kirwan and Smith they have the speediest outside men I know in any one team, and once they get the ball they go straight ahead with the other forwards keeping well in line, and ready to take advantage of any opportunity which may be offered them. Brown, in the centre, is not particularly noticeable, in the sense that he is not flashy, but he passes out to his wings without the slightest hesitation, and runs in the confident expectation that it will returned to him. This is, I fancy, the reason he obtains so many goals. Cameron is a hard worker, and the most judicious member of the front rank, whilst Copeland plods away at inside left, and is always doing something or preventing an opponent from shining. The half-backs are a tower of strength. They may lack the finish of the United trio, but they are every bit as useful, and are continually on the job. If beaten they turn round and do all they can to harass their opponents. The only one to find fault with was Morris, who occasionally tried to be too clever, but is such a good worker that this little deficiency could be forgiven. The backs were all right, steady and sturdy, with always the primary object of clearing in view. Clawley I consider to be an admirable goalkeeper. Once in the first half he fisted away a shot, only to have it immediately returned, and it was getting dangerously near when he rushed into a pack of Sheffield players, picked up the ball at risk of great personal injury, and sent it well down the field. I have seen the United show better, and certainly more effective, football than they did on Saturday, and particularly in the second half. Taken as a whole, their forwards were superior to those of Tottenham, and as a quintette showed better combination. But it struck me they hardly displayed their accustomed dash. Bennett was unfortunately hurt alter putting in a magnificent shot during the first half, and this injury doubtless affected his subsequent play. At half-back they were fairly good, with Johnson the best of the lot. Needham had an injured toe, and hardly did himself justice. But the weak spot in the initial portion of the game was at full-back, for both Boyle and Thickett took unnecessary risks, and were often beaten by the speedy extreme wing men. In the second portion, no fault whatever could be found with either Boyle or Thickett, but previously neither them showed that desperate earnestness which is a necessity in final tie. Foulke was all right in goal, and had one or two nasty customers to deal with, whilst he had also to keep his weather eye upon the impetuous Tottenham forwards, who were not afraid of charging the United giant.

RESULT: TOTTENHAM HOTSPUR 2 - SHEFFIELD UNITED 2

TOTTENHAM: Clawley (goal); Erentz and Tait (backs); Morris, Hughes and Jones (halves); Smith, Cameron, Brown [2], Copeland and Kirwan (forwards).
SHEFFIELD UTD: Foulke (goal); Thickett and Boyle (backs); Johnson, Morren and Needham (halves); Bennet [1], Field, Hedley, Priest [1] and Lipsham (forwards).
Referee: A. Kingscot

Sheffield's second goal, which sent the tie to a replay, was somewhat controversial with opinion divided in the aftermath of whether or not the ball had crossed the line. The 'London Daily News' gave, perhaps, the most lucid description though without expressing any opinion on the matter: "...Lipsham centred, and Bennett headed the ball in. Clawley got to it on the ground, and Tait was also at hand, trying to clear, with Bennett attempting to force the ball through. The ball was eventually got away, but the referee ruled that it had crossed the line."

Before the final, the Everton F.C. enclosure at Goodison Park, Liverpool, had been the venue selected in case of a replay, but when this did indeed become necessary the Liverpool F.C. objected in consequence of their top of the First Division clash with Notts. Forest at Anfield Road on the same day. In view of the chaos likely to be caused by two high profile matches in the same City on the same day the F.A. decided instead to award the cup final to Burnden Park in Bolton. Should a further match be necessary, the Molineux Grounds, Wolverhampton, on Monday the 29th were chosen.

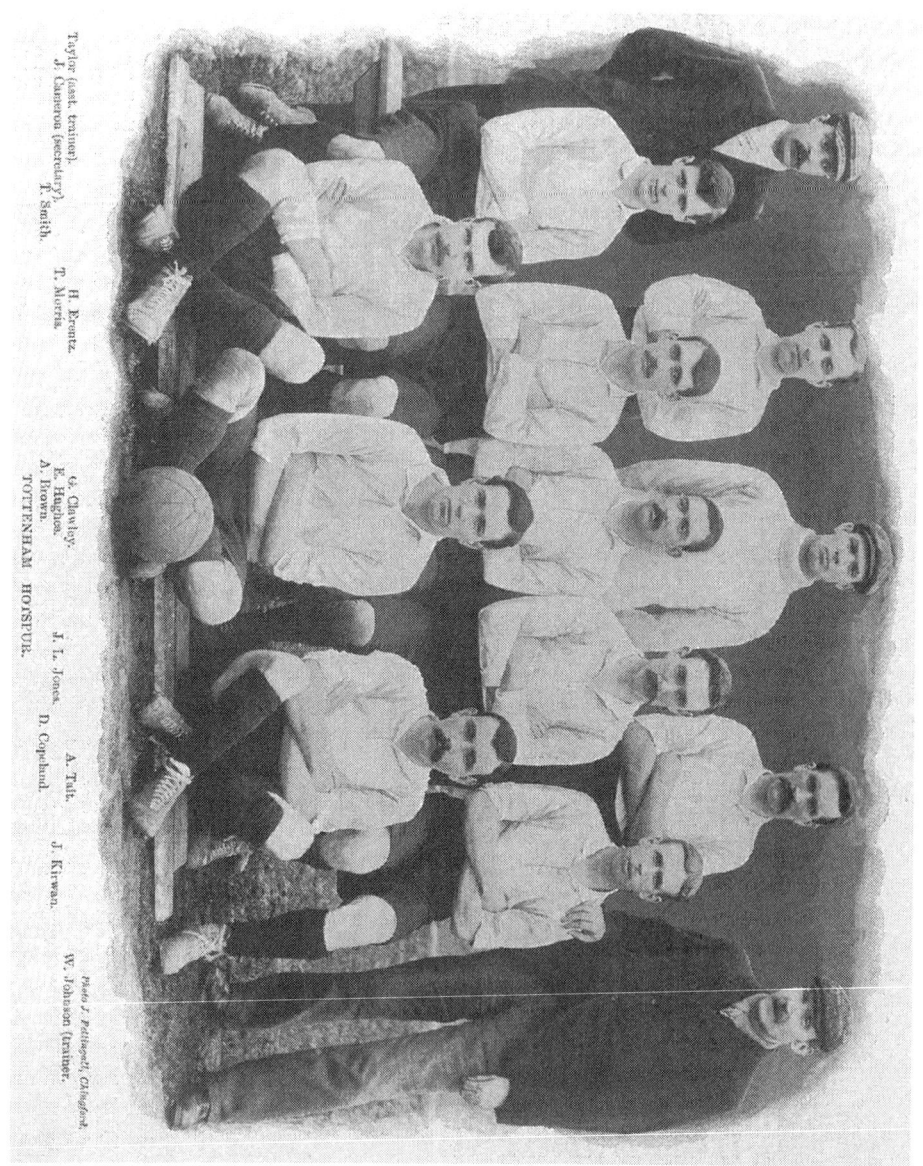

Taylor (asst. trainer). H. Erentz. G. Clawley. J. L. Jones. A. Tait. *Photo by* Pettingell, Chingford.
J. Cameron (secretary). T. Morris. E. Hughes. W. Johnson (trainer.
T. Smith. A. Brown. D. Copeland. J. Kirwan.
TOTTENHAM HOTSPUR.

Hedley. Morran. Johnson. Thickett. Beers. Field. Boyle. Priest.
Bennett. Foulke. SHEFFIELD UNITED. Ingham. Needham (captain).
Photo Jasper Redfern, Sheffield.

The Crowd Assemble

The Kick-off

A near thing for 'Spurs

A high kick

A cross comes in

Spurs emerge with the ball

Foulkes kicks clear

Clawley minds his charge

ASSOCIATION CUP FINAL.—(Special Sketches by Our Own Artist). 114,000 People at the Crystal Palace. Witness a Drawn Game between Sheffield United and Tottenham Hotspur.

THE GRAPIC - April 27th, 1901

Clawley avoids Bennett's charge

A good run by 'Spurs outside-right

Tottenham's second goal

S.T.DADD.

TOTTENHAM HOTSPUR v. SHEFFIELD UNITED
Final Replay – Saturday 27th April, 1901
at Burnden Park, Bolton
Athletic News - Monday 29th April, 1901

ABOUT THE GAME.

"FOR TWAS A FAMOUS VICTORY." Yes, I think it will go down history that Tottenham Hotspur's triumph over Sheffield United on Saturday by three goals one was one of the very best performances ever accomplished in a Cup final. Their superiority over their opponents was not so early made manifest as was the case when Bury ran Southampton off their legs in the first 20 minutes of the corresponding game twelve month back, but it had been demonstrated with almost equal force before the end of the afternoon, and there was no doubt as to which was the better side. Just for a moment I bid you glance at the table which is set forth elsewhere at the doughty deeds of the "Spurs," or the "Hottentots", as I love to call them, from the days of the first round. We thought Bury an immense team last year. I did. Well, they were an immense team, and knowing how things were with them before they set out on that destined-to-be illustrious campaign, and having followed them with peculiar kind of interest, I felt as proud of Bury as if I had been a full fledged "Shaker" or guarantor at the bank. Opportunities 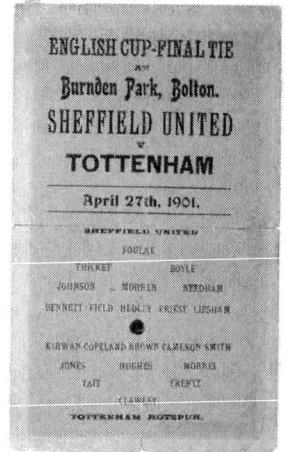 of watching Tottenham at exercise have been necessarily circumscribed, but I have at odd times seen sufficient of them to make me like them, and now I like them better than ever. In other words I rejoice that after all these years they have in fair and honest battle beaten our Northern champions at their own game. They are a cosmopolitan crowd, of course, and I don't suppose that any member of the team hails from within a hundred miles of London. Birth restrictions not counting with the majority of clubs which have carried off the coveted bauble, the success of Tottenham, however, must rank as a great Southern triumph, and leaving with a good deal of pleasure the Fleet-street brethren of the quill to stroll into the conservatory, one might say, and give full play to those rhapsodies in the exercise of which they are such past masters. I shall be plain and matter of fact and say at once that the result of Saturday's game will be to the benefit of football in general. Notwithstanding the flourish of trumpets with which the advent of the professional was hailed in the South, football in those parts can well do with such a stimulus as an English Cup victory will give, and desirous for one of seeing the game in the very first class spreading to all parts. I am hopeful that the success of Tottenham following the great work of those pioneers of progress who dwell at Southampton will stimulate others to similar endeavour. There is nothing like healthy rivalry, and 'tis well that the honours should not always belong to members of an exclusive set. An abundance of room prevails. Let talent, therefore, come forward and fill it. Here, if I chance to forget doing so later on, let me congratulate most heartily the Hotspur club and it's set of players on thus reaching one summit of their ambition. They seem to be good sports these gentlemen whose postal address is "London, N." I recollect - last season, was it - when they were beaten at Preston - a little party of their followers on the stand joining together, with hats waved on high, in a "three times three" for their conquerors, North End. The little ceremony was as pleasing as was novel, and I thought that afternoon that if luck ever did come their way they would deserve it. In the hour of triumph on Saturday, and as they were setting out for the station on their homeward journey, they must have been equally impressed with the home send-off which the inhabitants of Bolton gave them. They know something about football at Bolton, and in various fashions let the Hottentots have their candid opinion of the afternoon performance.

THE SPECTACLE AT BURNDEN

In some respects the affair was not a brilliant success. Bolton, of course, with it's paradise of bricks and mortar, compares but little with the verdant slopes of Sydenham as the venue of such a classic battle, for it's "park" at Burnden exists only in the imagination, and flanked as it is on all sides with emblems of commerce, the picture it presents is to some extent gloomy and artificial. It was quite time, however, that Lancashire was honoured with a Cup final, and Bolton, as the chosen site, stood well by its sponsors. Unfortunately, it was a case of making great preparations for people who did not come. There was accommodation for fully 40,000, yet little more than half this number availed themselves of it, circumstances apparently conspiring to keep the crowd down to these small dimensions. Alarmist reports that the ground would not hold the people, a suspension of cheap bookings into the town on the local railway service, double prices at the gate, and the prospect of not being able to see the game at that; all this kept away thousands of people who would like to have been present. There was thus no call for the troop of mounted policemen which had been engaged, no work for the firemen who were in readiness attach hose-pipes to the water mains and play on any obstreperous portion of the assembly. Many excursion trains were cancelled, others stopped on the way, and the few passengers they were carrying transferred to the ordinary services, and at night in Bolton the Beautiful there arose an unanimous wail from the proprietors of houses within the meaning of the Act[12] of a great slump in comestibles. They had laid out to victual an army, and the thing reminded one of the rich man's feast where many were bidden, but where the waiters had to search for customers in the highways and byways with fish-hooks, so to speak. No; after all the Palace beats everything else.

ABOUT THE GAME

With only a handful of sympathisers from London behind them the Tottenham players were not in such great esteem among the crowd on stepping out, but they speedily ingratiated themselves into popular favour when the ball had been set rolling, and a fair idea of how the game went in its early stages may be gleaned when it is said that for nearly half an hour Clawley had no work to do. Certes[13] the Southerners by winning the toss gained whatever advantage accrued from a choppy wind which blew diagonally, and such tall kicking were their backs able to indulge in without any trouble, that it seemed an imperative necessity that the forwards should score this half to do the team any good. But somehow they failed to get a mastery over the ball when the supreme moment arrived. Several hard drives from Brown, Copeland, and Jones, while going straight and true, were warded off more through good luck than merit on the part of the defenders, and Foulke had to come out meet some others which escaped the ruck in goalmouth, but reasonable chances were neglected, and when the United did at last get under weigh they were, even with fewer opportunities, the more dangerous. Thickett, from full back, was actually firing away at Clawley on one occasion, and it has to be said that this was a much better attempt to score than some which were made by presumably crack marksmen on the Sheffield side. However, a little bit of skirmishing around on the part of Needham led to Lipsham obliging with a pass to the centre, and the last-named partner completed a pretty movement with a shot just inside the post which gave Clawley no chance whatever. Hereabouts it should be said that the wind had dropped, and when the Hotspur came out to face the second half, a goal in arrears, they suffered no such handicap as the United had been labouring under for the first half hour. Having a weird recollection of two previous Cup-tie occasions in Lancashire when the Tottenham team after the interval, simply made the enemy look like many inanimate barrels I looked for events to transpire at the Sheffield end, and they were not long in coming, for the "Spurs" got first run, and twice a score looked imminent. But six minutes after the change **Cameron** fastened on a ball twenty yards out, and with a hard drive beat the giant in goal all ends up, and the teams were now on level footing. It was now that the war was at its hottest, and for a quarter of an hour a rare up-and-a-downer it was. Ever so little luck might have meant a score at either end, and the United came the nearest to accomplishing their ends. Their efforts to score, however, were for the most port puny. Clawley had one or two awkward customers, and a ball from Hedley, which glanced off Tait's back, all but caught him unawares. The attack, however, was gradually beaten back, and the result of another invasion of the terrace end was that Cameron tried another shot, pretty much the same as that which had scored earlier on. This time the ball deflected from its course, but it

---

12   Public houses.
13   archaic = certainly, assuredly.

came out to **Smith**, who made no mistake, and with a quarter of an hour to go Tottenham held the lead. They well deserved their success, but it looked like being discounted the next minute, as Priest arrived in front of Clawley apparently in undisputed command. Up came Erentz, however, and down went the Sheffielder just as folks were counting on him equalising. The fate of the Yorkshiremen was by no means sealed yet, although there were periods when their half-backs were simply run round. However, eight minutes from the close, and from a series of corners taken almost in succession, **Brown** at last found his chance to keep level with his previous Cup-tie exploits. Smith put the ball well across, and with a stupendous effort the Tottenham centre got his head at it, and it glanced into the rigging. I thought it the beet goal of the day, and it won the Cup right enough.

REMARKS

I have only once seen Sheffield United to such poor advantage, and that was during a series of home matches, in which their form, or the absence of it, suggested that they were labouring under some Satanic influence. The ground, perhaps, was not as they would have wished it, for somehow they have always appeared to me best when plugging away through the dirt. That first half hour of battling against the wind may also have told its tale, although judging from the length of some of Foulke's goal kicks, the breeze was not wholly in favour of the Southerners. Anyhow the United were a well-whipped team. There was no count to be laid against Foulke for the disaster. Ponderous and active man though he be, he had not midget's chance with any of the three balls which beat him, and I have seen him perform such valiant deeds that the spectacle of the giant being rendered helpless so many times is in its way a kind of treat. Still, with scoring opportunities the odds should always be in favour of the man in possession. Nor could it be said of Thickett that he did not play his part well, although he had a tendency to roam. And Needham was very nearly if not quite the best man on the field. He was not too sound starting, and was banged about mercilessly at times - once though did enact the "old soldier" - while Cameron and Brown between them kept him on at full stretch. But he was up with them at the finish, and if his shooting had only been fit to match with his other work the United would have had a much better time. Thus three men in the defence were proof to Cup-tie criticism, but the other members of the United rearguard were very much below par, and as Needham could not do three men's work the half-back line was simply cut into shreds at times. Of the forwards, Lipsham was hardly to be seen, Field little better, Bennett the Surprise - and a painful one - of his friends, and Priest and Hedley the only real workers of value. I did hear it declared, and by very influential and disinterested occupants of the grand stand, that when Priest scored one of his side had knocked the ball down with his hand. I didn't see it. Anyhow, it does not matter now. Tottenham's superiority was sufficient to allow this concession. The Southerners will declare that they won right enough last week, and Mr. Bullock and one or two of the team would, I suppose, for my satisfaction, have gone before any commissioner of oaths in Bolton on Saturday evening, taken the Book in their right hands, and sworn most solemnly that the ball which Mr. Kingscott said was over the line at the Palace was at least eighteen inches off. Not being present, your worships, I have been able to offer no opinion. On Saturday, however, the margin was wide enough, and quite satisfactory. Tottenham were superior throughout, and whereas there were many weak spots in their opponents' ranks, there was only one comparative failure on their side, for Smith alone seemed off colour, though Kirwan was now and again remiss. But for the most part the team were the masters in defensive tactics. The backs and halves gave no quarter, and once or twice their vigour outstepped bounds. They were full-hearted, however, rather than malicious, and they fairly broke the opposing attack in pieces, Erentz shining triumphantly. Equally successful were the forwards, whose passing movements quite took the palm among the scientific features of the day's play. Copeland, for his never-ceasing industry, and Cameron for his generalship were the pick, but the Queen's Park man, who seemed full of scheming, filled the eye better, and I imagine that he has played few better games. In the way of incidents there were two which I liked above everything else. One was a back-handed save of Clawley's. who had barely got back to his post from arresting an ugly rush; though as it happened no goal would have counted had he missed, for Mr. Kingscott had signalled a foul. The other was the terrier-like way in which Brown wriggled to the front and applied his head to that last corner kick when Tottenham booked their third goal. It was a goal in a hundred.

RESULT: TOTTENHAM HOTSPUR 3 - SHEFFIELD UNITED 1

TOTTENHAM: Clawley (goal); Erentz and Tait (backs); Morris, Hughes and Jones (halves); Smith [1], Cameron [1], Brown [1], Copeland and Kirwan (forwards).
SHEFFIELD UTD: Foulke (goal); Thickett and Boyle (backs); Johnson, Morren and Needham (halves); Bennet, Field, Hedley, Priest [1] and Lipsham (forwards).
Referee: A. Kingscott

A FEW COMMENTS.
[By Harricus]

In my opinion there was no question as to which was the better team - the one that won the Cup - so that whatever injustice they may have suffered, or imagine they have suffered, at the Palace, has been made good with interest. With the wind in the first half they ought to have done better than they did, for though Clawley did not touch the ball in defence of his goal until midway through the half, they did not make use of their chances. Luck was certainly in favour of the United, for Foulke got rid of many good attempts to score, and the United goal, by which they led at half-time, was not one to go wild about, though it was well worked for. I thought Needham was going through on his own, but he suddenly changed his mind, and crossed over to Lipsham, who placed to Priest, to add still another point to his goal crop. The United were certainly the smarter side in the later stages of the first half, their methods being likely to be more successful than the passing in front of goal, which the "Spurs" indulged in.

THE "SPURS" TO THE FRONT

Of course, the wind dropped in the second half, which was to the "Spurs'" advantage, yet it was by pure merit by which they obtained their three goals. Cameron got the equaliser in about seven minutes; Tom Smith, the leader, just after the half hour had struck, and the third came from a corner placed by Smith and headed through by Brown some five minutes from the end. There can be no denying the fact that after Cameron's goal the United were fairly outed, and, as Lord Kinnaird said at the conclusion of the game, there can no harm done in the Cup once more making the journey to London. The Association President spoke as a Southerner truly. Yet the game was one which was well enjoyed by the crowd, who, I may say, were most impartial, and, considering that their natural sympathies were with the United, as a League club, the winners had no reason to complain of the support accorded them. There were not 500 people from London, so that the "Spurs" required some shooters. The work of the goalkeepers was very one-sided, for, as compared with Foulke, Clawley had a very idle time of it. The giant custodian was at his best, and his efforts at kicking off from goal generally resulted in the ball landing in the other half of the field, and his punching was as effective as an ordinary player's kick.

WITH THE WINNERS

Tait played a clean game at back, and was the safer man of the two, while the half-back line played that worrying game which prevents opposing forwards working out cut and dried movements, and Captain Jones, as an old United player, must have felt very proud indeed when he received the Cup from the hands of his Lordship. The forwards were much ahead of the quintette representing the losers, and, as on the occasion when I saw them in the replay at Preston. I thought the left wing was the most effective. Copeland is a worker, and Kirwan was the best outside man on the field. Brown played a good inside game with Cameron and Copeland, though tor a man of his reputation I should have liked to have seen him shoot oftener. His vis-a-vis tried hard to keep his confreres in hand, but with the exception of Priest they did not rise to the occasion. The outside men were particularly weak, for Lipsham did not get across any centres, and Bennett gave us none of those brilliant flashes we know he is capable of. He was, too, very unfortunate with the ball, the passes being a little too short or out of reach, and several times the leather went into touch instead of the direction of Clawley.

THE BEST MAN ON THE FIELD

The one man of the team was Needham; indeed, I will go so far as to say that he stood out as the best man the field, and as compared with him Johnson and Morren were very small fry indeed. He was fairly in the wars too, though I must say the game was conducted in a splendid spirit. Thickett played a fine game at back, and he and Tait were the best couple, for Boyle made mistakes at times. Foulke could not be blamed for the defeat by any means, notwithstanding that in the two matches he has had five goals scored against him. He was at his best. Had he not been. Tottenham would have scored more goals, that's all.

THE PRESENTATION OF THE CUP
The Sportsman - Monday 29th April, 1901

This pleasing ceremony was witnessed by a fairly large proportion of the crowd, and was performed by Lord Kinnaird, the president of the Football Association, who stated that Sir Redvers Buller much regretted his inability, owing to another engagement, to be present. In his remarks the noble lord referred to the pleasure he felt at the trophy returning South after an absence of 18 years. In the stoutly contested game at the Palace the previous Saturday, in which honours were fairly divided. On the present occasion, however, the Tottenham team had proved themselves superior - at any rate, in the all important matter of goals, though he must congratulate the Sheffield captain and his men on the determined struggle they had made. They always played a sound, a hard game. Lord Kinnaird then, amid loud applause, handed the cup to the southerners skipper, J.L. Jones, who made a brief reply, inaudible to the crowd, in which he expressed the pleasure they felt as a professional team in having been able to take the cup back to the South. The gold medals were presented to the winning side, and before the proceedings terminated Mr. George Harwood, M.P. moved a vote of thanks to Lord Kinnaird, which was passed with musical honours.

THE RECEPTION OF THE NEWS AT TOTTENHAM

The victory of the 'Spurs was received at Tottenham[14] with tremendous enthusiasm, the crowd present at the Southern League match cheering the team again and again. Although a goal to the bad at half-time, they never lost faith in their favourites, and when it became known that the north Londoners had vanquished the First Leaguers to the tune of three goals to one there was no mistaking their feelings. Few were prepared for such a decisive victory, and for some time many seemed inclined to doubt the correctness of the news. Then it was announced that Brown, the champion goal getter this season, had been responsible for all three points, and there was another outburst of cheering. Altogether it was a sight that will long remain in the memory of those present. This evening, at the 'Spurs ground, arrangements have been made with the Prestwick Manufacturing Company for a grand display of animated pictures, showing numerous exciting scenes and incidents in the Cup-tie at the Palace and Bolton. Having won the cup, the directors of the club have also decided to wind up the affair with a firework display, so that some lively scenes may be expected tonight on the return of the team from Luton, where they are due to play a Southern League match.

TRIUMPHAL RETURN OF THE TOTTENHAM TEAM

Mafeking night was put in the shade on Saturday, or, rather, the early hours of yesterday, down Tottenham way, when a magnificent reception awaited the team who had been successful in bringing back with them the cup. They travelled back to town by the 7 p.m. special special train from Bolton, and reached South Tottenham shortly

---

14 The day of the replay clashed with 'Spurs home Southern League fixture against Gravesend. The game went ahead with both clubs putting out reserve sides, the Gravesend first eleven also being spoken for elsewhere – the Charity Cup Final tie at Chatham. News from Bolton was relayed by telegraph and announced at ten minute intervals. The 'Spurs side defeated Gravesend 5-0.

before 1 a.m. For two or three hours a crowd had been assembling, amusing themselves during the long wait by waving aloft the Tottenham familiar colours, blue and white, until, when the team did arrive, there must have been fully 8000 present. The funeral cards had a ready sale, and patriotic airs were sung, while, when the heroes of the day appeared the bands struck up, rockets were let off, and the team and their officials, in proud possession of the cup, had a right royal reception. They eventually drove to their clubhouse, receiving a perfect ovation on the way, and it was dawn before Tottenham bethought of sleep.

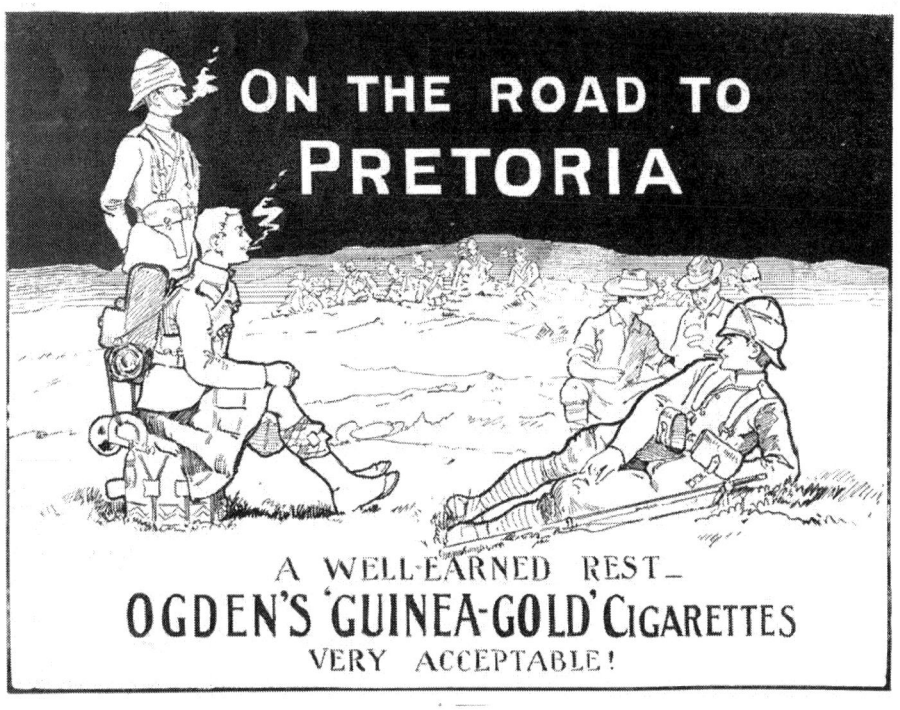

What Happened Next

The 'Spurs

In the Southern League, 'Spurs finished their cup winning season in 5th place, with Southampton resuming their accustomed position on top. The following season they finished second to Portsmouth, but would never repeat their championship triumph before departing the Southern League for the Football League under rather extraordinary circumstances at the end of the 1907/08 season.

The Championship race was extraordinarily tight that season, with 'Spurs solidly in the mix most of the way, although eventually only finishing seventh. At the beginning of April, 'Spurs, eventual winners Q.P.R., and displaced Northerners Bradford Park Avenue, each announced having made application to join the English Football League – the deadline for applications being the end of March (although the issue would not be resolved until the League A.G.M. in May). The Southern League had already lost several of their best members this way and responded by issuing an ultimatum to the three that they must withdraw those applications or resign from the Southern League by the end of the month – thus removing their safety net of continuing in the latter should those applications be rejected. Bradford promptly resigned, effective from the end of the season, but both 'Spurs and Q.P.R. questioned the legality of the order and refused to comply.

At the end of the playing season, the Southern League then scheduled their own A.G.M. to be simultaneous to that of the English Football League (at which new applications for membership would be decided upon). They also let it be known that the first order of business at their own A.G.M. would be a vote to expel 'Spurs and Q.P.R. for failing to comply with the order to resign. This placed both clubs in an extremely precarious position. To lose their Southern League status without gaining entry to the English League would be financially ruinous. In that scenario they would have been forced to go cap in hand to a lesser league to beg the dubious privilege of playing sides well below their own station.

At the last moment, Q.P.R. capitulated, their chairman, Mr. Walton, attending the Southern League A.G.M. and addressing the delegates there to the effect that his club had withdrawn their application to the English League, which would not now be voted upon. Bradford and Tottenham, meanwhile, pressed forward at the English League A.G.M. and presented their cases for election to that body. The matter of election to the Second Division was then put to the vote with the following results:-

Grimsby Town (applying for re-election) 32 votes
Chesterfield (applying for re-election) 23 votes
Bradford (Southern League) 20 votes
Lincoln City (applying for re-election) 18 votes
Tottenham Hotspur (Southern League) 14 votes
Burton United (Birmingham League) 1 vote
Queens Park Rangers (Southern League) withdrew

Rotherham Town (Midland League) withdrew

Consequently, with three places at stake, Grimsby and Chesterfield were re-elected, whilst Bradford took the place of Lincoln City. Tottenham, fifth in the voting, then missing out.

At the Southern League A.G.M., meanwhile, the vote to expel **both** Spurs and QPR, despite Q.P.R.'s last minute back-down, went ahead and was carried by an overwhelming majority. In Q.P.R.'s case it was pointed out that they had been given a deadline of 30th April by which to commit to, or resign from, the Southern League, and that that deadline had not been met. Thus Spurs and Q.P.R., two of the South's best footballing clubs, having failed to gain entry to the English League, were expelled from the Southern League and left without an alternative competition to play in.

The expulsion of two of it's best clubs from the Southern League caused a furore in the press - made all the more extraordinary, in Q.P.R.'s case, by the fact that they were the current Southern League champions! The English League at this point were prompted to start making plans for a Third Division, into which Spurs and Q.P.R. could be incorporated, and invited applications from other clubs - the deadline being June 10th. Fourteen applications were received, mostly from clubs in the English League's old stomping grounds of the North and Midlands. Spurs, applied, but not Q.P.R., who chose to pin their hopes on going back cap in hand to their old Southern League comrades. The plans for a new division were ultimately shelved, however, due to not enough of the applicants being of a sufficient calibre.

A new lifeline was thrown to Spurs and Q.P.R., however, on June 17th when Stoke City sensationally resigned from the Second Division, creating a new vacancy. Q.P.R. again chose not to apply and the vacancy eventually went to Tottenham. Q.P.R.'s show of contrition to the Southern League, meanwhile, eventually bore fruit when that organisation, at an Extraordinary General Meeting on June 22nd, voted to take the Rangers back in and extend the League to 21 clubs. Since the next seasons fixtures had already been published at that stage, however, and it was decided they were not to be interfered with, Rangers would have to play virtually all their games in midweek - drastically affecting their income.

'Spurs meanwhile, having scraped into the English League by the skin of their teeth, made the maximum from the opportunity, finishing their first season of League football second in the table, just one point behind leaders Bolton Wanderers. Second place, however, was good enough for promotion to Division One and so to complete 'Spurs journey to establish themselves among the elite in English football.

The Cup

The trophy that was presented to 'Spurs after their victory in the 1901 Cup Final continued to be used until the 1910 tournament. At that time it was discovered that the 1909 winners, Manchester United, had had an exact copy made to keep as a permanent presence in their trophy cabinet. Not prepared to accept the existence of a rogue duplicate, the F.A. then chose to retire the trophy and commission a new one, taking care this time to copyright the design. The new trophy, designed and manufactured by the Bradford firm of Fattorini and Sons, was first awarded in 1911, and it's first winners quite appropriately were Bradford City. That is the trophy still in use today, although now in its third incarnation (ie. the second of two copies necessitated by wear and tear on the original). The old trophy was presented to Lord Kinnaird in recognition of his services to the F.A.

Following 'Spurs triumph the North and Midlands quickly clubs reasserted their dominance over the competition and it would be a further twenty years exactly before the Cup again found a temporary resting place in the South, the winners on that occasion being ...

Tottenham Hotspur! ...

TOTTENHAM HOTSPUR v. WOLVERHAMPTON WANDERERS
F.A Cup Final at Stamford Bridge – Saturday 23th April, 1921
Daily Herald - Monday 25th April, 1921
HOW THE SPURS WON
Better Class Team Than the Wolves
By "THE SCRIBE"

In spite of a curtailed railway service, the usual bedecked, boisterous and happy crowd turned up at Stamford Bridge on Saturday see the London Spurs and the Black Country Wolves contend for the Cup, and the heavy rainstorm which coincided with the teams' arrival on the arena did not check the enthusiasm. The King's greeting was commendably brief, and the Wolves led off against the blinding rain.

The Spurs' famous left wing was at once prominent, and soon forced a corner off Woodward, who deputised for the injured Baugh. From the flag-kick Bliss tried one of his expresses, but the greasy ball went high over the crossbar. Not to be outshone, Brooks, the Wolves' outside-left finished a solo effort with a hard centre that Hunter caught and cleared at the post. The teams were now settling down to a hard, dour game, and the unusual spectacle was witnessed of four men requiring attention at once - Dimmock and Gregory, Grimsdell and Burrill. Cantrell caused a thrill when he secured the ball in front of goal from a free kick, but his final effort was miserably weak. The Spurs seemed to rely too much on their left wing, and with Val Gregory playing an inspired game this seemed a mistake, although the defence was not always successful. Edmonds was always ready to try a burst down the centre, but Clay put him offside repeatedly, and thus play was largely confined to the Wolves' half. McDonald interrupted a succession of fine volleys by a bad miskick, and Lee had a glorious chance to forge ahead, but he dallied with his centre, and Smith cleared. Nicely led by Hodnett, Brooke sent in a tempting centre which Hunter intervened and cleared. The Wolves were now forcing the pace, and Edmonds was unlucky with one of his specials, which merely cannoned off Walters, who was playing a rare spoiling game. The storm had now ceased, but the conditions underfoot were deplorable, and the Londoners wisely slung the ball about from wing to wing. An advance by Banks seemed dangerous, and the Wolves went for him, leaving Dimmock unmarked in front of goal, but a skidding ball beat him, and half-time arrived with blank score sheet.

The Wolves made the running after the resumption, but Lea's centre lacked pace, and the goalie easily cleared; much more danger was threat when Edmonds came galloping along in his best style, but Clay made a beautiful clearance that deserved all the applause bestowed, and the Spurs took up the attack. The right-wing received the ball more frequently in this half, and an inter-passing run by Seed and Banks ended by

The Winning Goal

the latter turning over a square centre to **Dimmock**. The latter lost the ball in a tussle with a defender, but luckily secured it from a rebound off Woodward, and fired in a low hard oblique shot that beat George all ends up for the all-important goal. For the first time now we saw the real Spurs, and Bliss, on two occasions, and Banks went very near in the next few minutes. Marshall eventually sent Brooks away, and the latter easily beat Smith, but in facing Clay both fell, and the ubiquitous Bliss cleared as Edmonds and Potts rushed up. The Midlanders' attack soon fizzled out, and at the other end only a fearless dive by George prevented Banks converting a nicely headed pass by Bliss. In the next minute George was hopelessly beaten by Dimmock, who rounded Woodward with ease, only to see his shot scrape the bar and go over. For once in a while Edmonds escaped Walters, and in due course transferred Potts, for the latter send Brooks away; but the winger took too long to centre, and his effort was crowded out. On the next occasion Edmonds went solo, and only a determined rush by Hunter prevented the equaliser. The ball went behind for an abortive corner, whereas an inside forward should have followed up and scored. Burrill made a sad mess of an opening provided by Clay falling on the treacherous turf; but the Spurs were from now to the end clearly masters of the situation, although they only won the narrowest of margins.

RESULT: TOTTENHAM HOTSPUR 1 – WOLVERHAMPTON WANDERERS 0

TOTTENHAM: Hunter (goal); Clay and McDonald (backs); Smith, Walters and Grimsdale (halves); Banks, Seed, Cantrell, Bliss and Dimmock [1] (forwards).
WOLVERHAMPTON WANDERERS: George (goal); Woodward and Marshall (backs); Gregory, Hodnett and Riley (halves); Lea, Burrill, Edmonds, Potts and Brooks (forwards).
Referee: J. Davies (Lancashire).

THE END

I hope you have enjoyed reading this book as much as I enjoyed compiling it. If so, look out for more publications taking in-depth looks at other special seasons in vintage club Football, and/or send your comments to spurs@clangillan.uk.

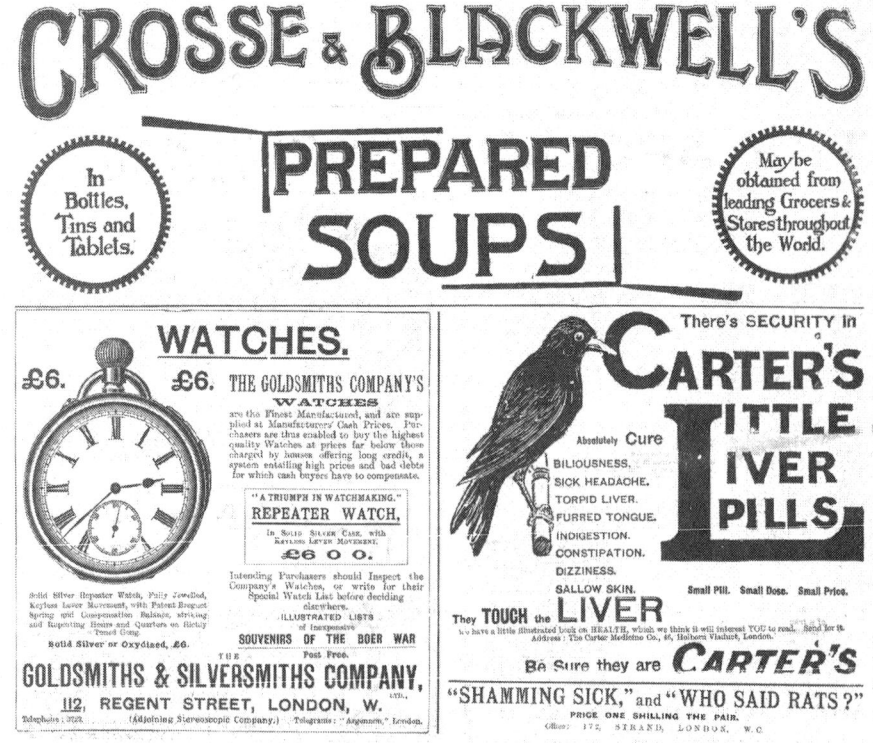

Appendix

The Complete Tournament

Preliminary Round: New Entrants = 40.

Tie no	Home team	Score	Away team	Date
1	**Eastbourne**	6–0	Worthing	22/09/00
2	**Darlington**	3–0	Tow Law	22/09/00
3	Sheffield	1–3	**Attercliffe**	22/09/00
4	Leyton	1–1	West Ham Garfield	22/09/00
4r	**West Ham Garfield**	4–1	Leyton	27/09/00
5	Turton	0–2	**Heywood**	22/09/00
6	**Olympic**	5–0	Upton Park	22/09/00
7	Stockton	0–2	**South Bank**	22/09/00
8	**Doncaster Rovers**	6–1	Rotherham Town	22/09/00
9	Norwich CEYMS	1–2	**Lowestoft Town**	22/09/00
10	**Bishop Auckland**	5–2	Stanley United	22/09/00
11	**Leadgate Park**	3–0	Crook Town	22/09/00
12	**Worksop Town**	3–2	Denaby United	22/09/00
13	Howden-le-Wear	0–2	**Darlington St Augustine's**	22/09/00
14	Hampstead	0–4	**West Hampstead**	22/09/00
15	Altofts	2–3	**Wath Athletic**	22/09/00
16	**Colchester Town**	7–0	Bury St Edmunds	22/09/00
17	Woodford	1–1	Leytonstone	22/09/00
17r	Leytonstone	1–10	**Woodford**	27/09/00
18	Great Yarmouth Town	1–1	Harwich & Parkeston	22/09/00
18r	**Harwich & Parkeston**	W/O	Great Yarmouth Town	
19	**King's Lynn**	2–0	Kirkley	22/09/00
20	Willesden Town	1–3	**Civil Service**	22/09/00

First Qualifying Round: New Entrants = 90, Previous Round = 20

Tie no	Home team	Score	Away team	Date
1	South Bank	0–3	**Thornaby Utopians**	06/10/00
2	Shankhouse	0–1	**Gateshead NER**	06/10/00
3	**Sheppey United**	1–0	Gravesend United	06/10/00
4	Folkestone	3–3	Sittingbourne	06/10/00
4r	**Sittingbourne**	W/O	Folkestone	
5	**Maidenhead**	W/O	Maidenhead Norfolkians	
6	**Civil Service**	4–1	West Hampstead	06/10/00
7	Druids	1–2	**Chirk**	06/10/00
8	**Blackburn Park Road**	5–1	Trawden Forest	06/10/00
9	**Newark**	6–1	Boston	06/10/00
10	**Oswaldtwistle Rovers**	4–0	Great Harwood	06/10/00
11	Burton Wanderers	2–2	Gresley Rovers	06/10/00
11r	Gresley Rovers	1–1	Burton Wanderers	11/10/00
11r2	Burton Wanderers	2–4	**Gresley Rovers**	15/10/00
12	Attercliffe	0–2	**Doncaster Rovers**	06/10/00
13	**Belper Town**	2–0	Heanor Town	06/10/00
14	**Workington**	4–3	Moss Bay Exchange	06/10/00
15	Darlington St Augustine's	1–1	Darlington	06/10/00

Page: 93

16	**Darlington**	4–1	Darlington St Augustine's	06/10/00
17	**Stourbridge**	5–2	Kidderminster Harriers	06/10/00
18	Tranmere Rovers	0–1	**White Star Wanderers**	06/10/00
19	Leadgate Park	2–2	Bishop Auckland	06/10/00
19r	**Bishop Auckland**	3–1	Leadgate Park	10/10/00
20	Mickley	1–2	**St Peter's Albion**	06/10/00
21	Chesham Generals	0–0	Chesham Town	06/10/00
21r	Chesham Town	0–3	**Chesham Generals**	11/10/00
22	**Rushden**	4–1	Desborough Town	06/10/00
23	**Worksop Town**	7–2	Montrose Works	06/10/00
24	**Ilkeston Town**	2–0	Stapleford Town	06/10/00
25	**Coalville Town**	3–1	Swadlincote	06/10/00
26	**Newstead Byron**	W/O	Hucknall Portland	
27	Swanscombe	0–3	**Grays United**	06/10/00
28	**Hinckley Town**	W/O	Nuneaton Town	
29	Middlewich Rangers	0–3	**Nantwich**	06/10/00
30	Wallsend Park Villa	1–1	Prudhoe	06/10/00
30r	Prudhoe	2–3	**Wallsend Park Villa**	10/10/00
31	**Crouch End Vampires**	3–0	London Welsh	06/10/00
32	Eastbourne Swifts	1–2	**Brighton Athletic**	06/10/00
33	Rothwell Town Swifts	1–3	**Finedon Revellers**	06/10/00
34	**Rochdale**	1–0	Rossendale United	06/10/00
35	Halesowen	1–2	**Brierley Hill Alliance**	06/10/00
36	**West Croydon**	5–0	West Norwood	06/10/00
37	**Rhyl United**	3–0	Llandudno Swifts	06/10/00
38	**Maidstone United**	4–0	Ashford United	06/10/00
39	**Richmond Association**	3–2	Shepherd's Bush	06/10/00
40	**Freetown**	3–1	Heywood	06/10/00
41	South Shields	1–2	**Morpeth Harriers**	06/10/00
42	**Birkenhead**	3–0	Buckley Victoria	06/10/00
43	West Ham Garfield	0–3	**Olympic**	06/10/00
44	Colchester Town	2–5	**Lowestoft Town**	06/10/00
45	Stockton St John's	0–2	**Thornaby**	10/10/00
46	**Wath Athletic**	3–0	Wombwell Town	06/10/00
47	Woodford	2–3	**Ilford**	06/10/00
48	**Grantham Avenue**	3–1	Grimsby All Saints	06/10/00
49	Royston United	1–2	**Hunslet**	06/10/00
50	**Brighton & Hove Rangers**	3–0	Eastbourne	06/10/00
51	**Godalming**	4–3	Redhill	06/10/00
52	**Mansfield Foresters**	2–1	Bulwell United	06/10/00
53	**King's Lynn**	2–1	Harwich & Parkeston	06/10/00
54	**Keswick**	3–2	Frizington White Star	06/10/00
55	**Earlstown**	3–0	Haydock	06/10/00

Second Qualifying Round: New Entrants = 18, Previous Round = 55

Tie no	Home team	Score	Away team	Date
1	Olympic	1–1	Ilford	20/10/00
1r	Ilford	0–2	**Olympic**	25/10/00
2	**Blackburn Park Road**	3–0	Oswaldtwistle Rovers	20/10/00
3	Morpeth Harriers	0–1	**Gateshead NER**	20/10/00
4	**Nantwich**	5–2	Winsford United	20/10/00
5	**Bishop Auckland**	3–0	Darlington	20/10/00
6	**Buxton**	Bye		

7	Stourbridge	2–2	Brierley Hill Alliance	20/10/00
7r	Brierley Hill Alliance	1–3	**Stourbridge**	22/10/00
8	Finedon Revellers	2–2	Rushden	20/10/00
8r	Rushden	0–1	**Finedon Revellers**	25/10/00
9	**Chesham Generals**	1–0	Aylesbury United	20/10/00
10	Worksop Town	0–0	Doncaster Rovers	20/10/00
10r	**Doncaster Rovers**	2–1	Worksop Town	25/10/00
11	**Ilkeston Town**	6–1	Belper Town	20/10/00
12	Slough	2–2	Maidenhead	20/10/00
12r	**Maidenhead**	3–0	Slough	25/10/00
13	**Gresley Rovers**	2–0	Coalville Town	20/10/00
14	**Oxford City**	Bye		
15	**Hinckley Town**	W/O	Loughborough	
16	**Hunslet**	4–1	Wath Athletic	20/10/00
17	St Peter's Albion	1–5	**Wallsend Park Villa**	20/10/00
18	Crouch End Vampires	0–1	**Civil Service**	20/10/00
19	**Grays United**	1–0	Sheppey United	20/10/00
20	**Oswestry United**	W/O	Ironbridge	
21	Rhyl United	0–0	Chirk	20/10/00
21r	**Chirk**	W/O	Rhyl United	
22	Maidstone United	2–2	Sittingbourne	20/10/00
22r	Sittingbourne	0–0	Maidstone United	24/10/00
22r2	**Maidstone United**	2–0	Sittingbourne	29/10/00
23	**Richmond Association**	W/O	1st Coldstream Guards	
24	Freetown	0–3	**Rochdale**	20/10/00
25	Welshpool	**W/O**	**Aberystwyth**	
26	**Thornaby Utopians**	2–1	Thornaby	20/10/00
27	Birkenhead	0–1	**White Star Wanderers**	20/10/00
28	Brighton Athletic	0–4	**Brighton & Hove Rangers**	20/10/00
29	**Yeovil Casuals**	6–1	Street	20/10/00
30	**Bristol East**	Bye		
31	Grantham Avenue	0–0	Newark	20/10/00
31r	**Newark**	4–2	Grantham Avenue	25/10/00
32	Hudsons	1–2	**Southport Central**	20/10/00
33	**Godalming**	4–0	West Croydon	20/10/00
34	Mansfield Foresters	1–2	**Newstead Byron**	20/10/00
35	**King's Lynn**	3–0	Lowestoft Town	20/10/00
36	Keswick	1–2	**Workington**	20/10/00
37	**Leighton Cee Springs**	W/O	Hitchin	
38	**Earlestown**	5–0	Swinton Town	20/10/00

Third Qualifying Round: New Entrants = 40, Previous Round = 38

Tie no	Home team	Score	Away team	Date
1	**Chesterfield**	8–3	Hunslet	03/11/00
2	**Clapton**	8–1	Maidstone United	03/11/00
3	**Darwen**	3–1	Nelson	03/11/00
4	**Kettering**	7–0	Finedon Revellers	03/11/00
5	**Watford**	10–0	Leighton Cee Springs	03/11/00
6	**Weymouth**	4–3	Yeovil Casuals	03/11/00
7	Marlow	3–5	**Chesham Generals**	03/11/00
8	Blackburn Park Road	0–1	**Blackpool**	03/11/00
9	**Southport Central**	3–1	Chorley	03/11/00
10	**Crewe Alexandra**	3–0	Stalybridge Rovers	03/11/00

11	Middlesbrough	3–3	Willington Athletic	03/11/00
11r	Willington Athletic	0–0	Middlesbrough	07/11/00
11r2	**Middlesbrough**	8–0	Willington Athletic	12/11/00
12	Lincoln City	0–0	Gainsborough Trinity	03/11/00
12r	Gainsborough Trinity	1–1	Lincoln City	07/11/00
12r2	**Lincoln City**	3–1	Gainsborough Trinity	12/11/00
13	**Chirk**	8–1	Welshpool	03/11/00
14	Burton Swifts	2–2	Newstead Byron	03/11/00
14r	Newstead Byron	0–4	**Burton Swifts**	07/11/00
15	Swindon Town	1–1	Bristol East	03/11/00
15r	**Swindon Town**	5–0	Bristol East	12/11/00
16	Shrewsbury Town	1–1	Walsall	03/11/00
16r	**Walsall**	1–0	Shrewsbury Town	08/11/00
17	**Workington**	W/O	Rochdale	
18	**Nantwich**	2–1	Buxton	03/11/00
19	Gateshead NER	0–1	**Jarrow**	03/11/00
20	**Stockport County**	6–2	Wrexham	03/11/00
21	**Newark**	2–1	Ilkeston Town	07/11/00
22	**Wellington Town**	W/O	Stourbridge	
23	**Gresley Rovers**	2–0	Wellingborough Town	03/11/00
24	Oxford City	0–4	**Reading**	03/11/00
25	**Hinckley Town**	2–0	Northampton Town	03/11/00
26	**Queens Park Rangers**	7–0	Fulham	03/11/00
27	**Staple Hill**	Bye		
28	**Wallsend Park Villa**	3–0	Hebburn Argyle	03/11/00
29	Grays United	0–2	**New Brompton**	03/11/00
30	**Barnsley**	2–1	Doncaster Rovers	03/11/00
31	**Brentford**	3–1	Maidenhead	03/11/00
32	**Oswestry United**	W/O	Coventry City	
33	**Bristol Rovers**	Bye		
34	**Richmond Association**	W/O	Wycombe Wanderers	
35	Thornaby Utopians	1–5	**Bishop Auckland**	03/11/00
36	Brighton & Hove Rangers	1–5	**Chatham**	03/11/00
37	Godalming	1–2	**Civil Service**	03/11/00
38	King's Lynn	1–4	**Luton Town**	03/11/00
39	**West Ham United**	1–0	Olympic	03/11/00
40	**Earlestown**	2–1	White Star Wanderers	03/11/00

Fourth Qualifying Round: New Entrants = 0, Previous Round = 40

Tie no	Home team	Score	Away team	Date
1	**Darwen**	2–1	Blackpool	17/11/00
2	Watford	1–1	Queens Park Rangers	17/11/00
2r	**Queens Park Rangers**	4–1	Watford	21/11/00
3	**Reading**	11–0	Chesham Generals	17/11/00
4	Chatham	2–2	Clapton	17/11/00
4r	**Clapton**	5–1	Chatham	21/11/00
5	**Southport Central**	2–0	Workington	17/11/00
6	**Middlesbrough**	3–0	Jarrow	17/11/00
7	Newark	0–5	**Chesterfield**	17/11/00
8	Chirk	0–1	**Walsall**	17/11/00
9	**Burton Swifts**	4–1	Hinckley Town	17/11/00
10	**Luton Town**	9–1	Civil Service	17/11/00
11	Swindon Town	2–2	Staple Hill	17/11/00

Tie no	Home team	Score	Away team	Date
11r	**Swindon Town**	6–0	Staple Hill	21/11/00
12	*Bishop Auckland*	5–0	Wallsend Park Villa	17/11/00
13	Stockport County	1–3	**Crewe Alexandra**	17/11/00
14	New Brompton	1–1	West Ham United	17/11/00
14r	**West Ham United**	4–1	New Brompton	21/11/00
15	**Wellington Town**	4–0	Oswestry United	17/11/00
16	Gresley Rovers	1–3	**Kettering**	17/11/00
17	**Barnsley**	1–0	Lincoln City	17/11/00
18	Brentford	0–1	**Richmond Association**	17/11/00
19	**Bristol Rovers**	15–1	Weymouth	17/11/00
20	Earlestown	2–3	**Nantwich**	17/11/00

Fifth Qualifying Round: New Entrants = 0, Previous Round = 20

Tie no	Home team	Score	Away team	Date
1	**Reading**	2–0	Richmond Association	08/12/00
2	**Walsall**	6–0	Wellington Town	08/12/00
3	Southport Central	1–1	Darwen	08/12/00
3r	**Darwen**	2–0	Southport Central	11/12/00
4	**Crewe Alexandra**	5–1	Nantwich	08/12/00
5	**Middlesbrough**	4–0	Bishop Auckland	08/12/00
6	Burton Swifts	1–2	**Kettering**	08/12/00
7	**Luton Town**	3–0	Queens Park Rangers	08/12/00
8	Barnsley	1–5	**Chesterfield**	08/12/00
9	**Bristol Rovers**	5–1	Swindon Town	08/12/00
10	West Ham United	1–1	Clapton	08/12/00
10r	Clapton	2–3	**West Ham United**	12/12/00

Intermediate Round: New Entrants = 10, Previous Round = 10

Tie no	Home team	Score	Away team	Date
1	**Chesterfield**	3–0	Walsall	05/01/01
2	Darwen	0–2	**Woolwich Arsenal**	05/01/01
3	**Kettering**	1–0	Crewe Alexandra	05/01/01
4	**Stoke**	1–0	Glossop	05/01/01
5	Reading	1–1	Bristol City	05/01/01
5r	Bristol City	0–0	Reading	09/01/01
5r	**Reading**	2–1	Bristol City	14/01/01
6	Grimsby Town	0–1	**Middlesbrough**	05/01/01
7	Burslem Port Vale	1–3	**New Brighton Tower**	05/01/01
8	Luton Town	1–2	**Bristol Rovers**	05/01/01
9	**Newton Heath**	3–0	Portsmouth	05/01/01
10	West Ham United	0–1	**Liverpool**	05/01/01

First round proper: New Entrants = 22, Previous Round = 10

Tie no	Home team	Score	Away team	Date
1	Kettering	1–1	Chesterfield	09/02/01
1r	Chesterfield	1–2	**Kettering**	13/02/01
2	Southampton	1–3	**Everton**	09/02/01
3	Stoke	1–1	Small Heath	09/02/01
3r	**Small Heath**	2–1	Stoke	13/02/01
4	**Reading**	2–0	Bristol Rovers	09/02/01
5	**Notts County**	2–0	Liverpool	09/02/01

6	**Nottingham Forest**	5–1	Leicester Fosse	09/02/01
7	**Aston Villa**	5–0	Millwall Athletic	09/02/01
8	The Wednesday	0–1	**Bury**	09/02/01
9	**Bolton Wanderers**	1–0	Derby County	09/02/01
10	**Wolverhampton Wanderers**	5–1	New Brighton Tower	09/02/01
11	**Middlesbrough**	3–1	Newcastle United	09/02/01
12	**West Bromwich Albion**	1–0	Manchester City	09/02/01
13	Sunderland	1–2	**Sheffield United**	09/02/01
14	Newton Heath	0–0	Burnley	09/02/01
14r	**Burnley**	7–1	Newton Heath	13/02/01
15	**Woolwich Arsenal**	2–0	Blackburn Rovers	09/02/01
16	Tottenham Hotspur	1–1	Preston North End	09/02/01
16r	Preston North End	2–4	**Tottenham Hotspur**	13/02/01

Second Round Proper: New Entrants = 0, Previous Round = 16

Tie no	Home team	Score	Away team	Date
1	Notts County	2–3	**Wolverhampton Wanderers**	23/02/01
2	Aston Villa	0–0	Nottingham Forest	23/02/01
2r	Nottingham Forest	1–3	**Aston Villa**	27/02/01
3	Bolton Wanderers	0–1	**Reading**	23/02/01
4	**Middlesbrough**	5–0	Kettering	23/02/01
5	**Small Heath**	1–0	Burnley	23/02/01
6	**Sheffield United**	2–0	Everton	23/02/01
7	Woolwich Arsenal	0–1	**West Bromwich Albion**	23/02/01
8	**Tottenham Hotspur**	2–1	Bury	23/02/01

Third round proper: New Entrants = 0, Previous Round = 8

Tie no	Home team	Score	Away team	Date
1	Reading	1–1	Tottenham Hotspur	23/03/01
1r	**Tottenham Hotspur**	3–0	Reading	27/03/01
2	Wolverhampton Wanderers	0–4	**Sheffield United**	23/03/01
3	Middlesbrough	0–1	**West Bromwich Albion**	23/03/01
4	Small Heath	0–0	Aston Villa	23/03/01
4r	**Aston Villa**	1–0	Small Heath	27/03/01

Semi Finals

Tie no	Home team	Score	Away team	Date
1	Sheffield United	2–2	Aston Villa	06/04/01
1r	**Sheffield United**	3–0	Aston Villa	11/04/01
2	**Tottenham Hotspur**	4–0	West Bromwich Albion	08/04/01

Final

Tie no	Home team	Score	Away team	Date
1	Tottenham Hotspur	2–2	Sheffield United	20/04/01
1r	**Tottenham Hotspur**	3–1	Sheffield United	27/04/01

Total Number of Clubs Entered: 215

Withdrew without Playing: 10
Withdrew after Playing: 5

WEBBS'

GOLD MEDAL COLLECTIONS
OF
VEGETABLE SEEDS

Containing liberal Assortment of the best kinds to produce a succession for Gardens of all sizes.

5/-, 7/6, 12/6, 21/-, 31/6, 42/-, 63/-, & 105/-, each.

From WILLIAM A. HUNT, Esq., Headbourne House, Jan. 16th, 1901.—"The collection of Vegetable Seeds is **the most liberal I have ever obtained, and I have tried all the leading Seedsmen.** The varieties are in nearly all cases those I would have selected."

See WEBBS' SPRING CATALOGUE, Post Free, 1s. Abridged Edition, Post Free.

WORDSLEY, STOURBRIDGE.

E. TAUTZ & SONS.

ORIGINAL HOUSE OF TAUTZ.

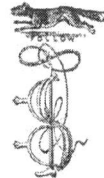

BREECHES MAKERS. **SPORTING TAILORS.**

Only Address:
485, OXFORD STREET, W.

Telegraphic Address: Buckskins, London. Telephone No. 3833 Gerrard.

CHAMPION & WILTON.
BY ROYAL WARRANTS.

STRAIGHT SEAT
SAFETY SIDE-SADDLE.

With Self Girthing Attachment. (PATENT.)

SORE BACKS PREVENTED.
DRAGGING BY THE STIRRUP IMPOSSIBLE.
Price complete, £13 13s. Net.

For Ladies who at all suffer from discomfort under the right knee through the pressure of the pommel, we make a Special Saddle, full particulars of which will be sent on application.

SPONGE-LINED PATENT NUMNAHS
FOR THE PREVENTION OF
SORE BACKS.
PRICES for SIDE or CROSS SADDLE.
No. 1. Of Leather, for Horses, hurt at the withers, as illustrated, 42s. net.
No. 2. Of White Felt, lined with Sponge at the back as well as at the withers, for horses that are galled under the seat of the saddle as well as at the withers, £2 10s. net.

In ordering, the length of the saddle from the back of the upright pommel to the cantle, and the width of the seat from edge to edge, should be sent.

Weston's Patent Safety Saddle Bars.
12s. 6d. per Set.

HIGHEST CLASS HARNESS.

457 & 459, OXFORD STREET, LONDON, W.

Nestor Gianaclis Cigarettes.
Made in Cairo.

OF ALL TOBACCONISTS AND STORES.

157a, NEW BOND ST.

CALLAGHAN'S
RACE AND FIELD GLASSES.

OPERA GLASSES,
Prices from **£2 10s.**

CALLAGHAN & CO.,
Opticians to H.R.H. the Prince of Wales.

23a NEW BOND STREET, LONDON, W.

ACTIVE SERVICE REQUISITES.

"THE PATH-FINDER."
(*Regd. Trade Mk.*)

Invaluable for Night Marching.

THE PATHFINDER. Sterling Silver Spring Hunter Complete with pearl dial and luminous points, especially adapted for night marching, £2 9s. 6d. In Gunmetal £1 1s. 6d.
Post free on receipt of remittance.

THE "CAMPAIGN" WATCH.
(*Regd. Trade Mk.*)

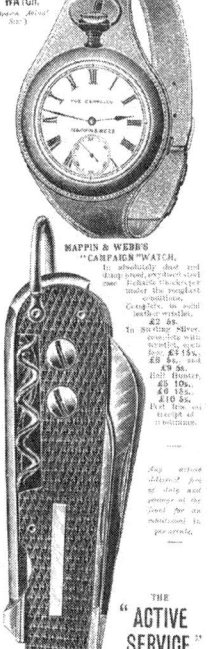

MAPPIN & WEBB'S "CAMPAIGN" WATCH. In absolutely dust and damp proof, oxydised steel case. Reliable timekeeper under the roughest conditions. Complete, in solid leather wristlet, £2 2s. In Sterling Silver, complete with wristlet, syn. keyless, £3 15s. £5 5s. and £9 9s. Half Hunter, £5 10s. £6 15s. £10 10s. Post free on receipt of remittance.

THE "ACTIVE SERVICE" KNIFE
(*Regd. Full Size.*)
Post Free, 17/9.

The "ACTIVE SERVICE" KNIFE (Brown's patent) with several forms of useful blades, containing large and small blades of best Sheffield steel, Corkscrew, Nail File, Gimlet, Hoof Pick, Tin Opener, two Screw Drivers, Pick, Tweezers, and Leather Borer, in Light Pigskin Case, with strap and buckle, and Khaki-coloured Lanyard. Complete, 17s. 6d. Post free on receipt of remittance, 17s. 9d.

MAPPIN & WEBB, Ltd.
(Chairman, J. NEWTON MAPPIN.)

ONLY LONDON ADDRESSES | 158 to 162, OXFORD ST., W.
2, QUEEN VICTORIA ST., E.C.

Manufactory:
THE ROYAL WORKS, SHEFFIELD.

Other Titles By the Same Author

Bradford City F.A. Cup Scrapbook 1911
How t'Cup Came Home to Bradford

The current F.A. Cup trophy is the second by design and the fifth by manufacture. The current design was created by the Bradford firm of Fattorini and Sons in 1911, and won for the first time by Bradford City - then only in their eighth year of existence and still their only cup win. This book relates the story of that remarkable triumph told through the press reporting of the period woven together into a cohesive story by the additional commentary of the author. How a brand new trophy, designed and manufactured by a Bradford firm, was first won by a Bradford Club. Includes the journey to the final of both finalists and the 'best of the rest' encounters from each round - teams, scorers and detailed match report of every match covered. Plus City's post cup winning Scandinavian tour told in greater detail than ever before.

Bradford City Season Scrapbook 1903/04 (inc. MANNINGHAM 1902/03)
Crossing Codes

In the summer of 1903 the Manningham Football Club made the momentous decision to give up the Rugby code and take up the Association game under the guise of Bradford City. This is the story of that transformation told through the period press and additional narrative by the author. Every game of both seasons covered: 1902/03 Manningham's last season of Rugby football; 1903/04 Bradford City's first season of Association football - stats and full period match report.

Bradford City Season Scrapbook 1907/08
Second Division Champions

Bradford City were unique in gaining entry to the Football League before they had ever played a single game or even raised a full team. Even so, after only four years existence they Championed the Second Division to earn a place among football's elite. Every game of that championship winning season covered - stats and full period match report.

Bradford Park Avenue Season Scrapbook 1907/08
A Southern Adventure

When the Bradford Rugby club determined to follow the example of their City rivals, Manningham (who became Bradford City) to switch to the Association code, their first application to join the Football League was rejected. Undeterred they applied instead to join the next strongest League in the land – the Southern League! This is the story of the club's first remarkable season among the southerners. Every match in Season 1907/08 covered - home and away - stats and full press match report.

Leeds United Season Scrapbook - 1919/20 & 1920/21: From the Ashes Paperback

An account of the origins of Leeds United from the rise and fall of Leeds City to the formation of Leeds United and a season in the Midland League before election to the English League Division Two. Every League and Cup match in interim period covered (stats AND match report): 1919/20 Leeds City, Division 2 (until disbandment); 1919/20 Leeds United, Midland League; 1920/21 Leeds United, Division 2. All this and more, e.g. interesting matches at Elland Road - Yorkshire Am. v. London Corinthians, Yorks and Lancs Ladies v. Dick Kerr Ladies and others.

Preston North End Season Scrapbook 1888/89
The Invincibles

1888/89 was the first ever season of the Football League competition. It was won by Preston North End. Not only did they win the League, they won the F.A. Cup that season also, making it the first ever 'double.' More than that, they won the League without losing a single game and the Cup without conceding a single goal! And all from a season comprising no less than 71 matches. This is the story of that amazing achievement, told through the press of the time with additional facts and commentary by the author. Every match of the entire season covered with period match report.

The First F.A. Cup (2nd Edition)

This book tells the full story of the Inaugural F.A. Cup Competition, from the establishment of the Football Association to the decision to create a national competition and the conduct of the first tournament. Every game in the tournament covered, including full press report, and details of the clubs involved. Also contains details of the first ever international match.

All of the above and future titles available through the Amazon bookstore.